Yearning

Authentic Transformation, Young Adults, and the Church

ROBERT HENDRICKSON

Morehouse Publishing

NEW YORK · HARRISBURG · DENVER

Morehouse Publishing, 4785 Linglestown Road, Suite 101, Harrisburg, PA 17112

Morehouse Publishing, 19 East 34th Street, New York, NY 10016

Morehouse Publishing is an imprint of Church Publishing Incorporated.
www.churchpublishing.org

Cover design by Laurie Klein Westhafer
Typeset by Denise Hoff

Library of Congress Cataloging-in-Publication Data

A catalog record of this book is available from the Library of Congress.

ISBN-13: 978-0-8192-2868-0 (pbk.)
ISBN-13: 978-0-8192-2869-7 (ebook)

Printed in the United States of America

*With thanks for the life and ministry of
the deaconesses of Saint Hilda's:*

Mary Johnson, Josephine Lyon, and Ruby Helen Thompson

*We ask for their prayers, that those who carry their
name at Saint Hilda's may also share in their living
witness to the Christ who came among us to serve.*

Contents

Acknowledgments

I AM RELUCTANT TO EVEN BEGIN with acknowledgments simply because it is so easy to forget someone when so many have been such a part of one's work. It is important that I begin by thanking those who have made Christ Church, New Haven the place it is over its history and today. Throughout these pages you will read many people's reflections on a place and people that have been vital in the Christian journey of so many. It is a curious and holy place full of brilliant, funny, quirky, and prayerful people who it was my privilege to serve. If you're ever in New Haven, Connecticut, do yourself a favor and stop in to take in not only its liturgy and architecture but to say a prayer in the midst of a place that seems a living embodiment of the beauty of holiness.

My thanks especially go to the interns of Saint Hilda's House and Ascension whose reflections you will read. I hope you'll hear the passion and commitment each of them has for sharing the gospel in deep and lasting ways. It takes courage to come to a new place, to commit to living in intense community with strangers, to encounter stories of brokenness each and every day in challenging work placements, to pray in a way that is unfamiliar and demanding, and to learn to express how God is moving in their lives in new and challenging ways. If leaders across our Church could look to their courage and self-giving and find themselves inspired, we would open ourselves to a movement of the Spirit that could only be described as a great awakening indeed.

I especially want to thank our intern (and now seminarian) Jordan Trumble who had passion and vision for this project and whose commitment to the power of Christian community comes alive in her reflections on these pages. I can only say to rectors looking for a curate in a few years—hire this woman! You'll have gained a woman of humor, insight, and energy who will help your parish grow in every way that matters.

In addition to our interns, three guest clergy have also contributed essays from their own experience. Erika Takacs, Steve Rice, and Bob Griffith are all priests of great dedication, vision, clarity, and energy. Their ministries inspire me and I am honored not only to have their contributions to the book but even more so to call them friends.

The dangerous temptation in many Church circles is to attribute the health or success of a place to one individual or another—a great priest or pastor or a stellar musician. Yet, I don't think it would be amiss to give a gentlemanly nod to David Cobb, the rector of Christ Church, whose leadership and presence have brought Christ Church into a new era of engagement with the city and beyond. As a new priest, it is easy to fall prey to one camp or another, to this method of ministry or that. Father Cobb does not let one forget that prayer is at the heart of the Christian life, of ministry, and of the Church as a whole. His combination of knowledge, care, spirituality, humor, and talent make him a mentor who has formed countless men and women for ministry in deep and lasting ways. Those who serve with him will learn to pray, read scripture, celebrate the Mass, and more, all with deeper understanding of just how God is with us in those moments if we can only get out of the way.

It would be a great scandal if I did not mention just how much the editor of this book, Sharon Pearson, has provided energy and guidance at crucial moments along the way. Despite my own relative disorganization, she kept things moving along and deserves much credit for its completion.

Finally, my deep apologies and thanks to my wife, Karrie, who has heard me say, more than once, "Well, in my book . . ." We are never prophets in our own house and I think that may be because those who love us must hear all of the trial versions of every prophecy (and also hear all those that don't come to pass).

To those I have forgotten—when the next book comes along just remind me so that I might write something truly profound and tear wrenching in your honor.

Foreword

WHEN CONVERSATIONS MOVE FROM THE larger culture into the Church's orbit of concerns, or when the reverse happens, it often means the question is played out. There is the topic "spiritual but not religious," which is beginning to wear thin. There is the constant anxiety-driven need to discover what will "save" the church as numbers decline—or the effort to pretend numbers do not mean much. Given the weight of attention that has shifted to blogs and social media, particularly as a point of working out positions and predictions and prescriptions for the future of the Church, there is something remarkably stable and enduring about a book. The last message I read about the "spiritual but not religious," or that post that made so much sense out of the absence of young adults in the church, swiftly sinks into the distance—just before I get my comment ready to post.

Though it will abide on bookshelves for an extended period of time, this book is a witness and an account of a moment in time and of a particular constellation of people, many of whom are parts of a particular community with its own history. It grows out of what people have discovered as they have sought to know and follow Jesus Christ within the life of the Episcopal Church, mostly through one parish and its worship and commitment to discernment with young people. This church has also been a leader within the Anglo-Catholic movement and then within the progressive side of that movement. This book grows out of a conversation just as real, though much slower, than the ones that keep us at our screens and keyboards.

Christ Church, New Haven is known for a profound and beautiful liturgy enriched with deep respect for beauty as an expression of human dignity in response to God. Splendid music, carefully thought-out movements that allow multiple ministers to move without confusion, and an abundance of incense—incense we make ourselves—are the obvious markers for which we are known and respected in some places, in others, not so much. They are the obvious markers, but they are not, to quote James DeKoven, "the thing itself." Not many years ago, after a particularly involved and spectacular ordination held here, a diocesan staff member said to me half-joking, "Now I know I'm not an Anglo-Catholic." My response was quick, "That's not what being Anglo-Catholic is about." It's not the incense or the vested subdeacon, the chanted Gospel or the polyphonic setting of the ordinary in Latin.

"Come back Monday morning at 8:00 a.m." was the answer I gave. That is when a lay reader opens the building and as homeless folk drift in and a few people take their place in the chapel, Morning Prayer is said. It could be the head of the English Department who begins, "O Lord open thou our lips" but the response, "And our mouths shall show forth thy praise" may come from a resident in a nearby halfway house. The person we do not recognize could have loved someone dying in a nearby hospital, now looking for strength and comfort in familiar words. It could be that the stranger is someone who has never been in a church before. For most of the year, a dozen or so young people—interns from the Episcopal Service Corps House or seminarians—will be there. Scripture and psalms, speaking eloquently or in baffling and disturbing histories; the collects that shape the year for anyone who follows the Book of Common Prayer; and the canticles that turn our minds to God—these things will be read. Most mornings they will be heard and taken to heart; at other times they will gently pass us by. Occasionally they will change lives. We trust they are heard and received in the presence of God. That is the thing itself—a trust that the structures we have been given are useful and that when we speak our praise and make an offering of our prayers, they are heard. Discipline and delight come together in patterns and well-crafted collects. Trust in God lets us mumble the Office when we are distracted or weary, just as it lets us come with full hearts and soaring spirits, knowing that we are not speaking into a void. Again and again, what is offered is our longing for God and our trust that God longs for us. In these acts of worship and in the community that builds up around them and then goes on to witness and serve, there is a longing that is answered and that continues: to find and be found by God.

Christ Church would be a profoundly different parish if it were located merely a few hundred feet from where it is. We stand at the edge of a campus and of downtown, at the edge of an academic neighborhood and the edge of another neighborhood of immense need. Our history has given us a pattern of sacramental focus and creedal theology that leaves us conscious of standing at the edge of the kingdom in its fullness, and our awareness of ourselves and others leaves us on the edge of all that is noble and all that is heartbreaking in humanity. Part of this life on the edge leads this parish to respond particularly to young adults—to those seeking out the path that leads them toward God and into lives that matter. Flimsy theology and worship that is constantly self-referential will, like so much of our chatter, be ephemeral and endlessly ironic in its self-consciousness. Reverence before the mystery of God's grace and patience to think through doctrine, to pray through the liturgy in its fullness, and a commitment to something greater than our own fleeting impressions and feelings is compelling and responds to a deep hunger within. This book gives an account of how several different people have experienced this place—and others like it—as points where desire and longing are shaped toward God and find fulfillment.

What we aim for is not the "pretty"—the decorated or the trendy. It is beauty that matters. And that word encompasses any work that reflects human dignity and the innate goodness of creation. Beauty is not confined to the useful, but it does speak of purpose—of the deep purpose in all things and in all people—to reflect the glory of God. What we strive for is not to be relevant or to catch the wave of current imagination, but to speak as truly as possible of what we have heard of God and know of ourselves. We are not "creating community" but being drawn into the "blessed company of all faithful people." The mystical Body of Christ is a spiritual reality of cosmic dimensions that we know as a few people who nod or briefly speak to each other after Morning Prayer or who have grown in friendship and common purpose for decades. To offer beauty that expresses truth within the common life of our mutual faith might not catch the wave of answers to anxieties about numbers, and it might not pick up on the ever-shifting jargon of social science, popular culture, and the media. But it rings true, not least to the young people who write in these pages and the countless others who pass through this place and through so many places like this.

At one of the most intense moments of the church year, just as Lent turns from penitence and renewal toward the mystery of Christ's passion, death, and resurrection, the collect for the fifth Sunday of Lent teaches us to pray for grace, that we may love and desire the things of God and that our hearts may find a place of constancy. While we need the conversation to continue in blogs and posts and tweets, while we need to ponder deeply what concerns arise within the changes and chances that will come later today and tomorrow, more than anything, we need to learn to desire and to love the promises and commands of God. We pray to love what God commands and desire what the gospel promises, because Christ has promised to abide with us and calls us to abide within him. The next wave of technology and the next important idea might either sell some new consumer good or reduce some human suffering to a spectacle for this news cycle. Some of it is pleasant enough and some of it is necessary viewing if we are to be informed citizens. This book—and the Church's mission—is about something different. What we do and what these people write about is simply this: how we shape our desire and our love for the things God commands and promises, and how Christ is forming in and among us a place where he will abide. That, as DeKoven would have said, is the thing itself.

David Cobb
Rector, Christ Church
New Haven, Connecticut

Introduction

Here We Are

RECENTLY, THE ANGLICAN COMMUNION HAS seen the enthrone-ment of a new archbishop of Canterbury and the Roman Cath-olic Church has seen the resignation of Benedict XVI and welcomed Francis as bishop of Rome. What has struck me with both men is their apparent longing to return the Church to some more essen-tial way of being. Pope Francis's emphasis on building a church of and for the poor and Archbishop Justin Welby's emphasis on evan-gelism and outreach seem to be striking a chord with their churches and with the wider world. Perhaps what is more striking about both is how "real" they each seem. They embody, in different ways, an authentic way of being a Christian leader in the twenty-first century.

Both men seem acutely aware that the Church is at a crucial moment (if it ever is not). Yet something deeper seems at work. There is a hope that both bodies might recover that which has always marked the Church at her most vital—an active and living engage-ment with the wider world grounded in service and loving evangelical witness. I think the Episcopal Church is at just such a moment. We are acutely aware, in many circles, that whatever we have been doing just isn't working anymore. We now have a chance to find a new and yet very old way forward that is built not on cultural assumptions, social expectations, or privilege but is something that can tap that most essential of desires—a yearning for a deeper relationship with the Triune God.

I firmly believe that our young adults can lead the way in this revitalization. In some ways, the task at hand is to figure out how to pass along the tools, traditions, and more that are essential to our identity and let them take the lead. The emerging generation is less invested in tearing down or even rebuilding. They are passionate about conserving, caretaking, and community. We are passing on to them a host of unsustainable ways of being. Whether it is environmental degradation, economic instability, international instability, and more, we are leaving them with a host of issues that represent a failure in leadership. Amidst that uncertainty, there is a powerful need for a Church that both announces Good News and creates a space of stable community that can call us to deeper mutual responsibility and love. The intentional communities that are bubbling up all over the Episcopal Church and other Christian bodies represent a chance to form workshops of new Christian life in which eager, faithful young people can find the vocabulary to express their longing for God and be formed in regular patterns of worship, service, prayer, and mutual care. They can be places where Christian leaders are formed who know what it is to live a life of love for God and neighbor with all they are.

The Church that we seem to be overreacting against in many quarters no longer exists. The lived experience of young Christians now embodies the very things that previous generations struggled to win. The pressing new cultural reality, though, is the utter indifference of youth and culture to the Church and the absolute irrelevance we have for too many young people. Yet we subject ourselves to round after round of self-fascination rather than observing the world that is actually unfolding around us and figuring out how to engage the emerging realities.

There were massive challenges that needed to be overcome in the '60s. Entrenched racism, oppression, and sexism were absolutely reflective of deep sin. Yet the tools and language of the 1960s are not what are needed half a century later. So much of our energy and time is devoted to revisiting the wounds of the past that there is no space or energy left to imagine the future. There are new Christian experiences and voices. If we think God is still speaking, then let God speak. Release the tie-dyed bonds and let God loose for a new generation.

The Church cannot afford to spend our days relishing the

glories or the struggles of the past or applying the dualistic, zero-sum thinking of the past to the future. We are going to have to be nimble, creative, and most of all deeply mindful that our root and common bond is in the new life in Christ rather than the old life of sin. Leadership with young adults requires a conviction that Christ is at work in new ways—the Church is relevant only in its offering of the conviction that Christ lives and promises that things that were cast down are being raised up. Our energy these days seems utterly focused on the traumas of the past rather than the hope of the future. We simply have to have the courage to stop trying to pretend that being relevant means aiming for the 1970s, 1980s, 1990s, or the '00s. Whether it is the business-speak of the '80s, the liturgy and music of the '70s, the social agendas of the '60s, the "emerging" church of the '90s, or the countless other ways we are trying to catch up, we are failing to look to the future and to be honest about where we are right now. We keep aiming for marks that have already passed.

This book is not about our institutions, our structures, our party affiliation, or our feelings—they cannot be our agenda. "We are not that interesting," says a priest friend of mine, "God is the interesting thing about the Church." We will only grow into our future as the Church when we reconnect with those essentials that define us, that are authentic to us, that make us matter as a Church. Young people are not looking for a cool Church or even a relevant Church. The whole culture is selling them cool. They are looking for a real Church—a Church that matters—and a Church matters only in the depth with which it offers authentic and profound thanks and praise in thought, word, and deed.

The challenge today is to focus on the world that is and is unfolding—looking outside ourselves and our walls to see where God is at work. Our young adults can do that ably for us if we can learn to listen. In the language of power analysis, it is time to give them some of our power and allow them to more fully inhabit this Church in which they are not an add-on to our lives but are themselves full members of the Body, claiming equal voice in its common life and witness.

Baptism gives voice in the life of the Church and we have young baptized members eager and able to pick up the yoke and carry the Church into the next decades. They have the passion, drive, and experience to open the Church up in life-giving ways that we could never have imagined and to make it powerfully relevant and alive. We have to listen, though. We have to invite them to speak. We have to give them the lectern, the pulpit, or the microphone and listen as they tell us how God is still at work in the world.

Hearing New Voices

This is the task of this book. To offer a space for young people that I have had the privilege of being in ministry with to share their experiences and hopes for the Church and to help us begin to simply trust that God is working in their lives and through their varied gifts. I've also asked colleagues to share a bit from their own mission fields and to reflect on how they see God's mission unfolding in the lives of the young people they work with as well. I am struck by the consistency across our parishes and cities and think something powerful is happening all around us if we'll simply have ears to listen.

Over the course of this book, we'll reflect on what gifts the Episcopal Church has in particular that place it in a unique position to address the needs and hopes of younger Christians. Readers from other traditions will also find within it hope for their own Christian communities and denominations as well, because these trends, as we will note, are happening across the Church, and every tradition has its own core identity that it can tap into to revitalize its common life.

There are a number of particular areas that seem to resonate with young adults. The chapters in this book grow out of reflecting on aspects of our common life that draw young adults in. Those areas—authenticity, beauty, tradition, rigor, catholicity, and mission—are all of one piece and it is a somewhat artificial distinction to draw any kind of clear lines demarcating one chapter or one concept from another. For example, how does one not speak of beauty when speaking of catholicity or not speak of rigor when talking about mission? Perhaps, however, what will come across is that authenticity is the common thread throughout the book. In each chapter there is a bias toward—or perhaps an algorithm of—authenticity. You will see it in the essays each of the young adults writes as well. One of the essayists concludes his piece with the simple line, "Christ Church is real." This lies at the heart of any work worth the reading, any community worth living in, any relationship worth pursuing—that it be real.

We have also invited reflection by a number of young adults who are part of this parish in one way or another. Most are interns with our young adult intentional community, Saint Hilda's House. Some are seminarian interns, parishioners, or former members. Each of them has found something here that has drawn, formed, and transformed them. I asked them to write a bit about not only the shape of our common life but also for our community members to reflect on how intentional communities like Saint Hilda's not only change individual lives but also can change the Church. I also asked them the simple question, "What are you looking for in a church?" and their answers are illuminating.

It is, in many ways, a snapshot of our life together. It is incomplete, as any snapshot is, and some details will be missing, some key element of the backstory untold, and some bits here and there that may confuse more than illuminate. Yet I hope that it is nothing if not an honest snapshot—something more like a candid picture of a family gathering when we see real joy revealed rather than one of those hazy, stilted, and posed glamor shots so many of our families have taken.

The goal of this book is not to figure out how to make the Church relevant. It is to explore how the living Christ is not only still relevant but is powerfully speaking in new ways that draw on our deepest, our most real traditions. In intentional communities of committed Christian young people, Christ is known and being made known. This is the flourishing of what Phyllis Tickle calls the "Ancient-Future Church."[1] We often refer to the Church as being in the already-not yet time of kingdom. I have never felt that more than now.

We are on the cusp of a something new in the life of the Church and it is unfolding around us right now. It will not look like what Church has looked like for the last century or so, but I think it will look very much like the first- and second-century Church. In many ways it will look like the Church of the Middle Ages. It will look like

---

[1] Phyllis Tickle, *The Great Emergence: How Christianity Is Changing and Why* (Grand Rapids: Baker Books, 2008).

the pioneer churches of the West, the schoolhouse churches of the South, the prairie churches of the Midwest, and the house churches of near and far. It will be gathered around campfires and altars. It will meet in basements, dens, naves, halls, bars, and parks. It will be baptized in fonts and rivers. It will bear life and know death.

In other words, it will look like the Church has always looked at its healthiest and most alive—like a group of committed, praying, hard-working people sharing in the life, death, and resurrection of Christ.

CHAPTER ONE

Spiritual Wandering

From Tourist to Pilgrim

OVER THE YEARS I HAVE developed a deep fondness for visiting China. I am especially fond of the Tibetan areas of the southwest in Yunnan and Sichuan Provinces. Among my favorite activities is to wander slowly through Buddhist temples and monasteries and just take in the ambience, the sights and sounds of a place suffused with prayer—that feels as if it is built of prayer. I marvel at the paintings and frescoes with their colorful array of fantastic creatures, multiarmed deities, and sometimes gruesome scenes of punishment. You have the sense that history is absolutely alive there and that you are walking in space beyond time.

When I first started visiting China and traveling to various monasteries, it was in a time of significant spiritual wandering in my own life. I was very much a literal and figurative pilgrim. As I wandered through, I was drawn by something. I was captured by a deep sense that here was something and someplace holy. Yet by the same token, I could not have told you much of anything about Buddhism. I did not have strong feelings for or against it. Buddhists seemed to have a language and structure that was entirely their own with a cosmology I could not penetrate and an artistic expression that defies the standard rules for artistic beauty.

I was drawn in, though. Eventually, through conversation with Buddhist monks, I was encouraged by them to go home, back to the tradition of my upbringing, and give it a try again. They were concerned that someone would come fleeing something else rather than simply being drawn by what they had to offer. That began a long return back to Christianity and into ordained ministry with the Episcopal Church.

The transition I made was, over time, from tourist to pilgrim. It is the challenge of the Church to create a space and encounter for the same to happen for the many, many wanderers who will come through our doors. We need a Church that expects people to be present not as consumers of an experience but as part of sharing in the encounter with Christ. We need churches that offer a shape to their journey so that we become a place of refreshment, protection, peace, and transformation. We are often quick to treat those coming to our churches as tourists—as consumers to whom we will offer a set of services designed to make their journey easier, more fun, and less complicated. Somehow, we seem to think, if we just lower the bar enough and make it accessible enough, they will stay. Yet this discounts the power of the journey—the richness of self-offering. Those coming through our doors are not necessarily looking for an easy faith—their lives are not easy and they need a faith demanding and complex enough to actually call them into newness of being.

> We need a Church that expects people to be present not as consumers of an experience but as part of sharing in the encounter with Christ.

My great privilege now is to work in a parish that offers a Sunday evening liturgy that is full of candlelight, chant, and incense and is as captivating for the senses as those visits to the monasteries. The young people I talk to (around 100 to 150 each Sunday night) are coming for reasons as complex and as vague as those that led me from temple to temple. Most of them have no real opinion about Christianity, one way or the other. They have not inherited the hurts that many of their parents felt in the Church. They are simply curious to come and see.

What strikes me is that when they enter, they often know as much about our symbols, art, language, and structure as I did about Buddhism. That which their parents rebelled against is for them only vaguely on the periphery or is actually their own form of rebellion.

The task has become not only to draw them into the building but into a relationship with Christ. This happens over time and with care—like any real relationship does.

A little about this place—Christ Church, New Haven—and its history and mission might be helpful. When we began our work with young adults, it grew out of the disciplined life of prayer and spirituality that forms the core of Christ Church's identity. One of our first steps was to look at our history to figure out where our deepest joy is found as a parish. In our history were a couple of key elements. First, we are a place of regular prayer. We say the Daily Office with regularity, praying on behalf of the whole congregation daily.

We hear confessions, offer daily Mass, believe strongly in the Real Presence, say the Daily Office, offer Benediction of the Blessed Sacrament, and hold Our Lady in high esteem. These are all integral parts of a Catholic faith that sustain this community. They point toward "the thing itself" which we hold dear—that we worship a living God that condescends to come among us. We also have women serving as priests, have long supported LGBT inclusion, and support a degree of freedom in matters of conscience such as birth control.

We embody, in manifold ways, the intertwining of the past and the future in a way that holds fast to that which is essential to our identity while drawing from that tradition to find new ways of welcoming those at the margins into the life of faith. We balance holy tradition with reason and scripture in such a way that the individual is neither left unmoored to their own devices nor denied the dignity of conscience. This life together is supported by the comprehensive underpinnings of a creedal theology and Prayer Book Catholicism.

The building is never empty, but always in use, even when there are few or no people around. The very stones of this building are always lifting prayer up. Second, we are a place of the Eucharist. Part of our founding was to offer Communion regularly. Who we are and how we live in the world around us is formed by our encounter at the altar. Third, we are a place of mission. We were established in a place called Poverty Square as a parish that offered free seating at a time when pews were rented. It continues to be crucial that who we are includes any and all who come and pray regardless of their status or ability to pay.

Growing out of those key marks of our identity, in 1910 Father

Frederick Burgess established deaconesses in habit (nun's garb) to be resident at Christ Church. They lived in a residence called Saint Hilda's House; they would serve the sacristy of the church, the children of the church school, and the poor and orphaned of New Haven until the early seventies, operating a free medicine clinic, soup kitchen, and many other ministries. In remembrance of their work and in that tradition, we have retained the name Saint Hilda's House.

As we began to form Saint Hilda's in its current form, we looked to our history first as a starting point. Having that history helps us articulate who we are authentically as a body. It gives us a distinctive way to engage the faith and help others to come and see something of Jesus expressed and encountered in the beauty of holiness.

We have also been a place, given our location in the heart of Yale University in New Haven, with a long tradition of forming people for ministry. Countless numbers of people have come through this place and been called into service in the Church in various ways. Recently a photo of me wearing a red chasuble from my ordination was online—we had a wonderful conversation trying to remember the many, many people who had been ordained wearing that same set over the decades here.

So we have a history of disciplined prayer, sacramental life together, service in the community, and forming young people for ministry. We have the model of the deaconesses offering themselves in community as they lived, prayed, and served for the glory of God. All of those elements are drawn together and we build on those things that mark who we are as a parish and give us joy. We formed Saint Hilda's House—a residential young adult community devoted to spiritual formation in intentional community in 2010. It is a community marked by regular prayer, spiritual discipline, corporate worship, and missional engagement in the wider city through their placement sites and community service.

Our interns come from across the country and many from backgrounds that are not Episcopalian. We are very clear that this is a program with a distinctly Anglican charism. It is designed to share that authentic expression of the faith that shapes and guides their corporate life. They live in a community in which there is little private space, minimal personal funds, with a high degree of structure in the schedule. The entirety of the program is designed to draw them out of themselves even as they get to know themselves more deeply through sacrificial living with others.

After looking at our history and identity, we began to put together a theological articulation of why we were doing this. What shape would our life together take? For us, it made sense for our life as a community to take on the shape of the Eucharist. We titled the curriculum *Life: Consecrated*. Its goal is to help our interns see how the Holy Spirit, which descends on common elements like bread and wine, making them holy things for the feeding of God's people, is present in their own lives and forming them to be the Body so that they may draw others to a living encounter with Christ. The whole of their lives is being transformed for holy work—consecrated to God's purpose.

The curriculum begins with considering how we come together and prepare for Mass. Who is coming together? Why are we here? What are we doing to respond to God's action in our lives? All of these are part of preparing for Communion. We make the move toward the offertory from there. As part of offertory, we consider questions of sacrifice and giving to God. Within both the preparation and offertory, we consider how we confess to God those things that may be blocking our experience of the Holy.

From preparation and offertory, we move to consecration. In many ways, this forms the heart of the curriculum as we consider how we are transformed to be part of God's action in the world. By grace, we come to be more of Christ, and are fed even as we learn to feed others. After consecration, we move to breaking and sharing. We consider this portion of the curriculum, which roughly corresponds to Lent, to be critical. In this section, we ask questions of doubt, hurt, pain, loss, and need and their impact on the life of faith. Finally, we come to the section on going forth. In this section, we summarize what we have talked about through the year and we discuss where the interns go from that point on in Christian living. We help them figure out how they will "Go in peace to love and serve the Lord."

These young people are looking for a faith that will demand their best and transform their lives. They are not looking for easy answers, vague spiritualities, watered- down theology, slipshod worship, therapeutic

They are not looking for easy answers, vague spiritualities, watered-down theology, slipshod worship, therapeutic relativism, private faith, or a monocultural God.

relativism, private faith, or a monocultural God. They are desperately searching for a Church that offers an encounter with the Holy that transforms, convicts, inspires, and draws them in.

They are searching for a Church that demands their best. Whether it is in mission, worship, theology, or daily life, they want a Church that is relevant not because it tries to tell them only what they want to hear, but because it offers them a vision of the Holy and its transforming power. A Church that reaches for and preaches relevance is a Church that makes itself irrelevant. The quest for relevance is the mark of quiescent extinction.

Questing for relevance, as if it is a goal worth achieving in and of itself, is a sad and tired pursuit. It is not relevance that defines a people or that marks transformational leadership, but authenticity, passion, and purpose. It is passion for God that shines through and marks a Church as Holy, as set aside for God's use, and as deeply and overwhelmingly relevant.

There is a profound difference between a Church that is "relevant" and a Church that matters. We are relevant only insofar as we offer a way for our believers to have their lives formed to the pattern of Christ's own life. We are relevant only insofar as we offer cruciform living and it is only in offering that transformation that we matter.

Young people are not looking for the easy path in life. They don't mind a challenge—it is too often us who fear the challenge. They are not looking for the path of least resistance. Look at the number of young people participating in the Occupy movement across the country or those joining Teach for America, the Peace Corps, the Episcopal Service Corps, Jesuit Volunteer Corps, Americorps, Lutheran Volunteer Corps, and the countless other service programs that call young people to live sacrificial lives in the service of others. These young people are not trying to find an easy path—they are trying to find a path that makes a difference both to themselves and to others.

The Church must honor that deep desire by offering more—by offering them all that we have ever had to offer—the life-changing encounter with Christ. Young people are searching for a way of being that is honest and rooted in something greater than themselves; the Church has been too timid about offering that. We can do so with joy, for we are part of a Church that has a way of being the Body together that honors individual gifts while also calling us to a higher common identity.

Many church meetings these days feel a bit like a wake for the Church:

> "Oh, I just remember the good times . . ."
> "You know, God has a plan for these things . . ."

I keep waiting for someone to say "It looks so peaceful . . . so natural . . ."

There is deep-seated fear, sadness, and a sense of loss that are palpable in the Church these days—and there are reasons for grief. Yet we are now tasked with moving on (grieving a bit) and getting back to the work of God. The world's need for news of God's love is too great for us to indulge in self-pity and strained good-byes to a Church that never really existed.

The only thing the Church has to offer and has ever had to offer is the worship of God who calls us to relationship. That worship is the heart of evangelism. It is the pulse of outreach. It is the essence of the history and future of the Church.

I am not talking of worship in the ritual sense—though that is vital too. I am speaking of something deeper, the turning of the heart toward God. This is what the Church is called to—turn its heart, the heart of its believers, and the heart of the world around us toward God. It is the genuflection of the heart in awe.

One of our teenagers, whose parents attend another parish, came to Christ Church because, as she told her dad, "The Prayer Book offers so much!" She was searching for a place that honestly tries to live into the fullness of our common identity as Anglicans. She was searching for a place that knows that the Church has so much to offer—and is part of the group of young people holding us accountable to offer it!

The next generation of church leaders is ideally prepared to bring the Church forward. They understand the complexity of human nature and society. They value honesty and real relationships (despite how we might disparage the falsity of Facebook and the like). They have a healthy approach to life that finds identity more in relationships than career. They have seen both the challenges of fundamentalist religion and the costs, especially to families, of a society without grounding. They are always searching for the real amidst hypermarketing. They are generally optimistic and not saddled with cynicism or with a reflexive distrust of (and desire to deconstruct) everything. They are trying to figure out how to put the pieces back together again.

In other words, they are prepared to lead a Church that is grounded, honest, thoughtful, optimistic, complex, and engaged. For those despairing for the future of the Church, I can honestly say that we have a generation of leaders coming who will make all of us very proud. However, we have to have the courage to pass on to them a Church that knows who and what it is. We will be deeply blessed as our leadership becomes increasingly intergenerational.

For these young adults, the social dislocation and rebellion of the 1960s are over. I have heard it said that many in the Church hope to wake up and have it be suddenly 1950 all over again when full buildings and bulging institutions were the norm. Of course this unhealthy impulse impedes mission and ministry. However, it is equally unhealthy to wake up and expect it to be 1968 all over again too. We have no more need for the Church of the '60s than we do for the Church of the '50s. We need to be ready for the Church that is actually around us and to hear the voices of young people calling us into new life.

Candlelight, Community, and Spiritual Hunger—*Jordan Trumble*

At 9:15 p.m. on my first Thursday of college at Capital University, a small Lutheran school in Bexley, Ohio, a young woman who lived down the hallway knocked on my door. She remembered me telling her during orientation that I am the daughter of an Episcopal priest and was active in my home church while I was growing up. She wondered if I would go with her to Candlelight, an ecumenical worship service that takes place each Thursday night on Capital's campus. Although I had personally resolved to try to stay away from church for a while when I went to college in order to distance myself from my parents' faith lives, my desire for friendship won out against my spiritual rebellion and I accompanied my new friend across campus to the chapel.

When we entered the chapel, it was almost completely dark; the only light came from a few candles arranged around the base of a tall cross and a projector throwing images of PowerPoint slides with song lyrics up onto the sloped ceiling. I spent the next hour singing and praying with my new schoolmates and, although I'd never planned on ending up in that chapel, the community I found there became a space where I would explore a variety of faith questions during the next four years. There were only a few Thursday nights of college that I didn't spend in that space; by the time I graduated, I had changed my major to religion, was active in campus ministries, played piano and guitar for the Candlelight music team, and was one of a handful of seniors asked to preach in chapel in our final semester.

It is only now, years later, that I understand what I first loved about Candlelight and what kept me coming back each week. While I enjoyed the music because it reminded me of the church camp I'd attended while I was growing up, I continued going to Candlelight because it was a community that was driven by the students. After the campus pastor gave a short sermon (what I would categorize as more of a blessed little thought than an actual sermon), we would break into small groups and pray together. The musicians would plan songs to sing, but we would also take requests or play whatever the Spirit moved us to play. And many weeks, Candlelight would end with a group of students continuing fellowship at a nearby restaurant. There was nothing prescriptive about what we did; Candlelight's community formed out of a desire to worship God with others and was constantly evolving to accommodate the needs and desires of those present.

After finding a spiritual home at Candlelight, I began searching for other ways of deepening my faith. I attended services at nearby Episcopal churches and Bexley Hall (an Episcopal Seminary), but still felt something was lacking. When it came time to schedule classes for my sophomore year, my advisor suggested trying some religion courses; I took her advice and enrolled in two religion courses, where I discovered a broad range of theologians who had written on community, from Thomas Merton and his writings on the monastic life to Shane Claiborne and his writings about The Simple Way community in Philadelphia. I made my way through stacks of books about community, liberation theology, and social justice.

When I read these works that spoke so passionately about community and with such conviction about the role of community in a life of faith, I was captivated. As I read the words of Oscar Romero, who was martyred for his work with the poor in El Salvador, I was forced to confront my own privilege. As a straight, white, middle-class young woman, the daughter of a teacher and a priest, I had never had to go without anything I wanted or needed. I had every opportunity set before me, and my view of the world was hauntingly narrow. I marveled out how someone could care so much about other people, and I was filled with questions. I wondered what my life meant and how I could make it more meaningful. I wondered how I could live more fully into communion with God and with others.

I wondered what my life meant and how I could make it more meaningful.

Instead of despairing and being wracked with guilt, though, I began to think and pray about my next steps. At the same time, I was writing my senior thesis on intentional Christian communities in the modern era, and had an idea. Why not expand my worldview by moving to a new city? Why not try a brand-new job? Why not live in community? Why not live in *religious* community?

I looked at residential internship programs from a variety of Christian traditions, but eventually decided to see what my own tradition did with the idea of community, so I joined Episcopal Service Corps. Three months after graduation, I moved to Los Angeles to be a part of the Episcopal Urban Intern Program. During my year in Los Angeles, I lived with five other young adults and worked at an HIV community center where I did everything from HIV testing at a local high school to outreach work with homeless young adults who slept on Venice Beach.

At some point between graduation and my moving back East a year later, though, I realized that working in a social service wasn't where my heart was and that although I loved the church I attended in Los Angeles, my soul felt a little empty. Although I'd been living in community with a group of fun, interesting, and compassionate people and went to church regularly, I craved a different sort of community and a different sort of spirituality. I had only survived that year by making regular lengthy phone calls to my best friends from college who had been inspired to do similar faith-based internship programs and by occasionally visiting with an old friend from summer camp that had moved to Los Angeles. I was feeling exhausted and spiritually deprived and, for as meaningful as that year was for me, I needed something else.

I yearned for a more ordered prayer life and more space to figure out where God was calling me. Amidst the bustle of Los Angeles, I'd found it hard to listen. As my year in Los Angeles came to a close, I started applying for other internships and jobs, but then I came across the website of the newly forming Saint Hilda's House community in New Haven. Like my internship in Los Angeles, it was a program of Episcopal Service Corps but had a slightly different flavor. In addition to community living and service work, Saint Hilda's offered daily ordered prayer time, spiritual direction, and weekly reading assignments and discussion groups. It sounded exactly like what I had been craving.

I spent the next two years at Saint Hilda's House, living and working with a total of twenty-one other young adults during that period. While the project of living in intentional community is rarely easy and is often actually quite difficult and stressful, the years I spent living in intentional community, in both Los Angeles and New Haven, were utterly transformational. On the other side of three years in intentional community, I have a different understanding of my own vocation, I engage the Bible and theology in new ways, and I have a radically different view of what it means to be in relationship with others; each of these changes could only come as a result of the experiences I had living in community.

So why does my story matter? What makes my story so special? Absolutely nothing. And that's why it's important. My story is probably not very different from the stories of many young adults you know. And although I am not a pollster and can't hand you scientific reports to verify everything I've said as being true, I feel quite confident in saying that many young adults have deep questions and spiritual needs and most of them are also seeking something to meet these spiritual needs. I don't need to read a study to know this to be true; the only studies I need in order to understand what it is like to be a young adult in the church are the conversations and relationships I have had with other young adults and the lived experience of being a young adult struggling with what it means to be a person of faith in a world that is plagued by violence and poverty. There is a spiritual hunger that is rampant among young adults and this hunger has driven many of us to the Church and, more specifically, to intentional communities in an effort to help quench this soul-draining hunger. Countless of my college classmates, friends from church, and childhood playmates followed a path similar to my own, living in community and finding new ways of encountering the Divine. Faith-based intentional communities offer stability, relationship, and discernment. But more than anything, they address this hunger, which, at its core, is hunger for authentic connection with other people and with God.

The idea of living in faith-based intentional community is attractive to young adults because it offers hope of relationship in an isolating world. With the advent of technology, we are able to connect with people on the other side of the world with a simple click, yet it is more and more difficult to make real-life connections with others. (If you are skeptical, I urge to take note of how many people are on their cell phones next time you are in a large public space.) This becomes even more difficult after one finishes school, which is the time when most young adults come to programs like Saint Hilda's House. Most young adults graduating from college have been in school since kindergarten and have no recollection of a time in their lives when they weren't in school where socialization is a natural process that comes about just simply by being around the same people week in and week out for months or years at a time. Life after graduation is radically different; many people move to new places and begin new jobs and have to make friends without the built-in structure that school provided. Young adulthood can be lonely and isolated.

Furthermore, my generation is coming of age in a time where every time we turn on the evening news or click on our Smartphone's news application, we are confronted by financial crises, ecological destruction, abuse, war, poverty, and famine. Of course, these problems have been around in various iterations since the beginning of time. Yet we are simultaneously, as a generation, more and more unchurched or de-churched. We are less equipped than previous, more churched generations to deal with the spiritual turmoil that comes as a result of growing up watching sexual assault trials and terrorist attacks on the television. Being unchurched or de-churched doesn't mean that the spiritual questions don't exist. Rather, they become even more pressing and often devastatingly difficult.

Intentional community offers space to explore spiritual questions in a supportive environment and a language and grounding for a life of faith that looks beyond oneself and toward the Divine. For me, this was the question of how I could live more fully into relationship with God and with others. Others ask questions of how the Church can address issues of injustice, or why a loving and gracious God would allow so many terrible things to happen in our world. These are never easy questions, yet community offers a space to be in conversation with and to learn from others, drawing us outside of ourselves. Programs like Saint Hilda's House don't shy away from difficult questions, but face them head-on, asking young adults to do the hard work of grappling with these difficult questions and, in return, offer support, guidance, and a safe space to learn about oneself and about God who calls us each into relationship with Himself and with all those we encounter.

Reflection Questions

- *Where have you been a pilgrim? A tourist? What was the difference?*

- *What do you seek in a faith community?*

- *Do you believe there is a difference between a church that is relevant and a church that matters?*

- *What should the church offer to individuals, the community, and the world?*

- *How could you live more fully in communion with God and others?*

- *What are you spiritually hungry for?*

CHAPTER TWO

Tradition and Relevance

Homecoming

A N ARTICLE THAT I WROTE in the summer of 2012, just before the
Episcopal Church's 77th General Convention, got an unusual
amount of attention. I posted it and found that within a few hours,
several thousand people had read, forwarded, posted it on Facebook,
and the like. The title of the piece was "Don't Do It for the Kids:
Of Hymnal Revision and Young Adults." I looked at a recent survey
conducted by the Episcopal Church about the possibility of revising
The Hymnal 1982.[2] The results of the survey were interesting, to say
the least. The survey result that most seemed to surprise people,
especially middle-aged Episcopalians, was that the group most resistant to hymnal revision was those under the age of twenty-nine—and
they were the most resistant by a large margin. The report concluded:

> Respondents in their twenties and younger
> are statistically different than the rest of the

---

[2] The Church Pension Group's Office of Research assisted the Episcopal Church's Standing
Commission on Liturgy and Music in fulfilling its 2009 General Convention mandate in
Resolution B004 to determine whether a revision of *The Hymnal 1982* was needed and wanted.
The full report of *The Hymnal Feasibility Study* can be read at www.cpg.org.

respondents, reporting the least interest in desiring worship music to reflect their personal musical tastes. This proves counter to the "common knowledge" theory that younger congregants are looking for a more modern or popular-music experience at church.

The report further stated that those "whose age is significantly above or below 50 are less likely to support revision. Middle-aged Episcopalians are more supportive of revision than younger and older Episcopalians." In the under-thirty demographic, lay respondents were 50 percent opposed to revision, 30 percent neutral, 20 percent in favor. Among under-thirty clergy respondents, 61.5 percent opposed revision, 7.7 percent were neutral, and 30.8 percent were in favor.

One twenty-two-year-old respondent to the survey put it this way:

> I think there is a huge assumption made that the younger generation wants guitar- and piano-based praise and worship music. . . . What we want to hear in a Sunday Eucharist are the classic hymns played on organ. And occasionally we want to chant. Church is the one place where our musical taste is not based upon fad, but instead links us with a much more important, more elegant tradition. If I wanted to listen to acoustic guitar and piano, I'd pick up Dave Matthews or Ben Folds. If I wanted rap, I'd listen to Lil Wayne. . . . For worship, I want music that connects to me a world outside of the in and out of my daily life.

While recommending moving forward gingerly with discernment, the report acknowledges, "That 13,000 people took the time to complete a lengthy survey on the question of hymnal revision shows how central *The Hymnal 1982* is to the life of The Episcopal Church. This should give us pause. A rush to revise the *Hymnal* could seriously undermine and weaken the Church, alienating those who have remained with The Episcopal Church through difficult times." The assumptions of many had been rather upended by the survey and the authors concluded, "Perhaps most significantly, there is no pattern in which youth correlates with a particular movement towards new forms of musical expression. To revise the Hymnal must in some way be a project that is a gift to the next generation. Gaining some clearer sense of what the worship music of that generation will look like will require a longer and more careful period of discernment."

What young believers are asserting, in different and manifold ways, is that there is a core to our tradition that they are craving. In effect, they are not looking for new, exciting, or alternative ways to be Christian but are returning to the forms that are at the heart of our shared identity. New Monastic movements, youth attending Latin Masses, a return to liturgical forms of worship in many evangelical churches, and the survey I wrote about all attest to something deep-seated that is taking place across the Church and our culture—young people are coming home. This homecoming, sadly for many of us in leadership, does not look like packed churches and stuffed budgets. It looks like something different—and something more profound. Young people are trying to return to a faith that expresses the essentials with conviction and passion. While middle-aged leaders talk of relevance, they are engaged in a dialogue with our traditions that we barely notice.

Young people are trying to return to a faith that expresses the essentials with conviction and passion.

Young adults, as the many stories in this book will attest to, are trying to find a space and place that is asking more of them. They are looking for a place that helps them be more defined in a culture of limitless self-promotion and so-called self-determination. This change is even happening in places far removed from our shores yet beset by the new pressures of consumer economy. In my visits to China, I am struck over and over by how young those visiting churches, temples, and monasteries are. They are a society whose undergirding social fabric has been upended by the rising of consumer capitalism, and young people there are finding new identity in worshiping communities.

Our own society is undergoing a similar sea change. It is now "ok" to not be Christian in a way that might have been unthinkable or unspeakable in previous generations. Yet I think it is more authentic. People are not crowding our churches because they have to or because it is expected of them. There is little social gain to declaring oneself Christian now. In many ways, the Church is facing a moment not at all historically unique. It must account for itself. Its excesses and abuses are now the stuff of public ridicule. From television evangelists and their foibles to the hyperaggressiveness of the religious far right (and the attendant media attention) to the clergy sex abuse scandals—religion has not done itself many favors in the last thirty years.

I am less baffled at the decline in religious attendance than I am that we somehow continue to stumble forward. I am surprised that the decline has not been steeper, faster, and more terminal. More Americans than ever may call themselves "nones" (those without religious ties), yet I am convinced that this is not because more Americans have suddenly fallen prey to atheism. I think that more Americans are simply willing to admit it. Yet I am equally convinced that in God's grace there is some identifiable core that remains and that can be built upon—and young adults are helping us find it. We have the opportunity to pair a deep and complex liturgical and spiritual life with a gracious and loving welcome that changes and transforms us as well as those we reach.

The space that Christ Church carves out is one that allows the sacred tradition of the Church to protect, shape, guide, and form young people into the Christians God is calling them to be. A parishioner of ours, reflecting on being a young LGBT person, spoke of his warm welcome to Christ Church: "This [acceptance] was felt by most of us [gay Christians] to be a radical proclamation. . . . One we would make with the defensive shield of extreme forms of ancient tradition all around us. We simply wanted to be counted as valued children of God, worthy of full recognition and acceptance by the Church." The fact that this welcome and proclamation took place within the context of the fullest traditions of the Church was not incidental—it was crucial—and it allowed him to see how his life was truly and utterly cherished by God. It allowed him to grow into an authentic Christian who also happened to be gay.

The passion of the young adults I work with is for authenticity—they want a place that demands that they grow into who God is calling them to be. Empty affirmation simply won't cut it— authenticity requires a conscious commitment and a community of prayerful purpose. It is something of a joke in hipster culture that there is a fetish for the real and the unique (the very fetish itself being the beginning of a movement that is somewhat un-unique). Yet that impulse—the desire to find the authentic—drives these young people in a powerful way. Even as they are pressured in manifold ways to conform, achieve, and excel—many of them know that something more is out there—and they are seeing it in us in ways we can scarce name. Thus the shock at the results of the hymnal survey; it was as if you could imagine readers of the results saying to themselves, "Us? You really like us?"

The thing is they do like us. When we are being authentic and not trying to market or sell them something. One of our young adult interns talks about an experience of gracious welcome she had at a parish with no one in their thirties or younger. She walked in as a nineteen-year-old and found a spiritual home with older worshipers who were totally comfortable welcoming her to their knitting club and tea. They prayed for her and asked for her prayers. They asked her to be part of their leadership, eventually, all the while trying not to awkwardly contort who they were in accommodating a newcomer. In other words, they were comfortable with who they were and made space for her to be comfortable with them.

She was one of the only young adults in that church—yet there are stories like hers across the Church. Young people coming home—searching for a place that reminds them of a place they have never actually experienced but know something of.

To the Tables Down at Mory's

As I write this, I am sitting at Mory's in New Haven, situated in the heart of Yale's campus. Mory's bills itself as a "Yale tradition," and it is. It is the kind of place that is tradition—where bygone days, decades, and centuries feel profoundly present. Yet it is remarkably alive. Its walls are wood paneled; its fireplaces warm; it is filled with pictures of Yale sports teams of years past—it is not unusual to spot a president here or a senator there in a jersey of some sort or another looking back in black and white; its tables are carved with memorials, initials, shorthand scrawl, college insignias, and more. It hardly elicits comment to find someone like Howard Dean or Robert Reich grabbing lunch there when they are in town. At lunch and dinner, the restaurant brims with both students and older patrons. In the evenings, it becomes positively raucous at times, with students stamping on the floors as drinking challenges are made over its famous "cups." The Whiffenpoofs, the oldest American collegiate acapella group, are a fixture here each night. In other words, it is a place where long-standing tradition meets newcomers every day.

Mory's has not always been this way. It began as a student hangout—a place for a gentleman to nurse a hangover perhaps with a bit of rarebit and baker's soup. Over the years, the atmosphere somehow became rarified. It seemed to trade on its status as a tradition rather than offer anything new—or really maintain the standards of the old. Its food was something to be tolerated rather than enjoyed. Its membership narrowed and its self-perception grew ever more self-referential. It enjoyed heady days in the first half of the twentieth century, retaining its connection to the students while becoming something of a marker of status for members. Yet as it grew more storied, it became an increasingly isolated place—seemingly unaccountable to the community around it and unable to change when needed. Eventually, it was forced to close, almost never to reopen.

It was thanks to a new vision of what Mory's could mean to the new generation of students and community members that it was revived. The interior was redone, a bar was added, professional chefs and management were brought on, and membership rules were relaxed such that it is now the largest "private" club in the country. Even more impressively, it managed to hold on to its longest traditions while still making the necessary changes to thrive in a new century—it is still most definitely Mory's. The Whiffenpoofs still sing, the baker's soup and the rarebit are still served (though the pickle tray has sadly been retired), and students still pass the night singing and sharing cups. Mory's now feels like it is alive yet steeped in tradition, rather than held captive to traditionalism. At the heart of this change is that Mory's is a place for students again—it found its new purpose in its original identity and by reaching back, it leaped forward.

The Episcopal Church has had a similar history. We started as something of an upstart with ties to upper echelons, we grew with a missionary spirit, we became an establishment choice that conferred status with membership, and then we lost our way. We became satisfied with providing a product of increasingly bland quality while trading on the memories of a bygone era. Yet like Mory's, the time has come to figure out who we are for the coming century. We can obviously no longer be a club with a narrow membership and limited access. Yet we also can't allow our whole tradition to be thrown out in the rush to redefine ourselves. Like Mory's, we have to commit to careful, thoughtful, and deep change—we have to rediscover who we were when we began—or we face a grim future. We have an opportunity to rediscover that which is essential to who we are and how we proclaim the Good News with integrity and authenticity.

Finding Home

When my wife and I first visited churches after moving to New Haven, our first stop was at a certain Anglo-Catholic parish. I walked out and said, "That is how church should be!" She said, "I am not going there!" She had grown up Methodist and the combination of chant, incense, and the like seemed to trigger her Protestant allergies. So we next visited a local Methodist parish. It was rather like a group meeting of some sort or another. There were lots of affirmations and story sharing while the faith component was conspicuous only because of its muted nature. We both walked out and said together, "I am not going there!"

Our third Sunday, we visited Trinity Episcopal Church on the Green. The welcome there was warm without being cloying. The music was beautiful. The choir that day was the Choir of Men and Boys. The liturgy was dignified without being self-conscious. It was Rite I (traditional language) Morning Prayer with hymns and anthems done with grace, dignity, reverence, and joy. In short, it was classically Anglican and my wife and I both fell in love with the parish. Communion there was Rite I East-facing (the celebrant facing the altar along with the people). We were both captivated and drawn in and found ourselves at home.

Without being able to name what we were looking for—we had found it. It was a place outside of our respective traditions and yet seemed utterly familiar (and yet unfamiliar). There were odd words to learn, lots of kneeling, newcomers groups, a Book of Common Prayer—each of these added to the sense that we were now part of something that mattered—that stretched back in time, was rooted in place, and knew who and what it was. It was a place that would shape and mold both of us in the decade that followed. Something else we noticed (and they noticed) was that the most traditional service offered was the most well attended and it continues to attract young families.

What we were yearning for, and what the young adults I now work with are striving after, is a Church that is faithful to its core—a Church that James DeKoven refers to as adoring "the thing itself." In a time of bitter controversy over changes in the liturgy (like candles, vestments, and incense along with substantial steps forward like prayers for the dead, and more frequent Communion), DeKoven spoke to General Convention and said, "to adore Christ's person in His Sacrament is the inalienable privilege of every Christian and Catholic heart. How we do it, the way we do it, the ceremonies which we do it, are utterly, utterly indifferent; the thing itself is what we plead for."[3] The thing itself is what young people are yearning for. Can they find a place that preaches Christ crucified, where they encounter him truly present in the sacraments, where they have gathered around them a community of pilgrims, where they are challenged because faith and life are challenging things? If they can find this, they will have found a home.

Tradition in the liturgical life is one place where this yearning can be seen and is the entry point, as it was for my wife and I, to a deepening life of faith. That tradition stands in for something—it is a sign of a place's commitment to the history and depth of the faith. It is by no means a guarantee! There are places with such liturgies that are absent of discernible Christian inquiry, service, or doctrine. Yet it is a way for young people to find something that feels

Young adults are yearning for a faith that is calling them to be more of the Body—to be rather than attend Church.

---

3 "The Canon on Ritual, and the Holy Eucharist": A Speech Delivered in the General Convention, October 26th, 1974, by the Rev. James DeKoven, DD, Warden of Racine College (New York: T. Whittaker, 1874), http://anglicanhistory.org/dekoven (accessed May 20, 2013).

grounded. It is up to us to prove that it is—that we are centered on the thing itself. In our community and parish—young adults are yearning for a faith that is calling them to be more of the Body—to *be* rather than *attend* Church.

Lest one think that this is a uniquely Episcopal phenomenon—it could be helpful to look at City Church in San Francisco. It is a Reformed church with few obvious ties to its parent denomination. On Sundays, they draw about one thousand people or so and they have several daughter congregations around the city. If you look at their worship bulletin, much is from the Book of Common Prayer 1979. They have regular Communion, celebrate the Triduum, and take part in the full life of the liturgical seasons. Brian McClaren's former church, a popular evangelical congregation, was a prayer book church. Shane Claiborne and Jonathan Wilson-Hartgrove make substantial use of the traditions of the prayer book. In other words, across sections of the evangelical churches that are often more in touch with cultural shifts and trends than mainline churches, there is a movement toward embracing that which defines who and what we are as a Church. The young people flocking to those churches are returning home.

The Episcopal Church's challenge now is not to be relevant—our approach to faith is utterly and completely relevant. Our challenge is to present the tradition freshly and with newfound commitment and vigor as we find new ways to preach "the thing itself." Relevance, for us, will mean living more fully into who we authentically are. The joy for us is that the elements of tradition proving so attractive in other places form us in unique and powerful ways—we live the reality of common prayer.

"Old" Is the New "New"—*Joseph Wolyniak*

I'll never forget walking into Wrigley Field for the first time—it was pretty close to a spiritual experience. I grew up a baseball fan. And as any good baseball fan would, I've visited my fair share of ballparks across the U.S. Most parks these days feature all the modern comforts and conveniences that fans have come to expect: plush seats, massive high-definition scoreboards, innumerable concession stands, waterfalls in center field, unwieldy playgrounds for kids (and their guardians) who find the gruelingly slow pace of baseball insufferable. Oftentimes there's so much by way of comfort and convenience that it seems attendees couldn't care less about the actual game!

But then there's Wrigley. Support beams for the upper deck obstruct field views throughout the park. The seats are a creaky, uncomfortable hardwood—that is, if you're not in the even-more-unforgiving bleacher seats. I'd rather forget what the bathrooms are like. Yet despite an antiquated stadium and perennially woeful record, the Cubs routinely rank in the top ten for attendance in the Major League. Anyone who's visited would understand. Wrigley is Wrigley. To step into Wrigley is to step into the world of baseball more-or-less as it was in 1914. Like it's ever-so-slightly older cousin (Fenway Park in Boston), Wrigley offers something that the newer stadiums cannot: history, tradition.

"Tradition" is often loaded with a negative connotation. For many, the word "tradition" can evoke an oppressive, exclusionary conservatism. It can be equated with those six words that can kill a church: "We've always done it this way." It can call to mind those painful instances when one was told—without a coherent reason—that they can't, shouldn't, oughtn't simply because they haven't, won't. For many, tradition evokes a nefarious tautology.

Yet when I think of tradition, I think of my grandmother—a farmer's daughter from Poland who emigrated to industrial Detroit in the postwar era, bought a house in the Polish borough of Hamtramck, and never left. She was a woman with deep Old World sensibilities. She lived in the automobile capital of the world but never owned a car—rarely even took public transportation. I don't think she ever touched a computer or cell phone. Her little nuggets of wisdom always came with a definite dissonance with respect to the modern world in which I lived. As a child, she was easy to dismiss: "Oh Baba, you have no clue." But the older I get, the more I realize that her Old World sensibilities represented a deep wisdom that enabled her to resist some of the trappings of our age. She was less captivated, captured by modernity. She was able to see the world in a way that I could not.

When I think about tradition, I think about our grandparents. I think about the very root of the word "tradition," which comes to us from the Latin *tradere*—literally meaning to give across time, to hand down, to transmit. I think about the wisdom that our grandparents hand down. I think about how much was handed down to me. I wasn't born nowhere. I was born into a particular family in a particular place. I was given a funny last name. I was baptized at St. Patrick's in downtown Detroit. I was marked, claimed, formed in ways that were not of my own choosing, in ways that make me who I am.

Such an understanding self runs against some deeply ingrained sensibilities in our American culture. Indeed, Episcopal theologian Stanley Hauerwas claims that Americans erroneously but instinctively believe that "we have no story except the story we chose when we had no story."[4] But if we think about our grandparents, we can think about the way in which our lives are caught up in a story that is bigger than ourselves. It's a story that starts with our mothers, our grandmothers, our great-grandmothers. And their great-grandmothers too.

That's what I think about when I think about tradition. I think about the stories that are handed down. I think about the wisdom that passes from one generation to the next. It is a wisdom that has to be mediated, to be sure. It is both impractical and imprudent to try to map Old World sensibilities wholesale onto the present. New wine calls for new wineskins. Focusing solely on the past can engender a useless nostalgia, or worse, an obstructionist traditionalism. We don't live in the Old World; we live in this world. The task before us is to receive the wisdom that has been passed down to us from ages hence and learn to—carefully, imaginatively—apply it anew in our time, this world.

This is no easy task. Just ask those early followers of Jesus who were faced with a real conundrum: All these Gentiles want to follow the Jewish Messiah, but should they really be allowed to join? Can we really break with thousands of years of tradition? We're pretty sure the Good News is for *us* (who've kept the Law, the sacred teachings of God, the wisdom of our foremothers and forefathers for generations), but can it really be for *them* too? Elders and apostles had to be consulted, councils convened, and sometimes the way forward can only

---

4 Stanley Hauerwas, *The Hauerwas Reader* (Durham, NC: Duke University Press, 2001), 250.

be discerned through unexpected dreams interpreted as divine messages, pronounced with an almost laughable assurance: "it seemed good to the Holy Spirit and to us" (Acts 15:28).

Negotiating the balance between tradition and innovation is and has long been a source of tension. The point, however, is not to completely do away with tradition, pretend like we can just make it up as we go along. The point is to receive the wisdom handed down, wrestle with it, apply it anew. Faithful reception of tradition requires re-formations. *Ecclesia semper reformanda est*: the church is always to be reformed. But, as Dorothy Day said, the Church always contains within itself the seeds of its own regeneration. Our grandparents—the Mothers and Fathers of the faith—are repositories of tried and true knowledge, perspectives and practices from the generations that have stood the tests of time, trial, and tribulation. We do well to take heed.

When my wife (Elizabeth Costello) and I, along with our friend Colin Miller, began dreaming up the Community of the Franciscan Way (now a mission of the Episcopal Diocese of North Carolina committed to community, prayer, and solidarity with the poor), one of the keys for us was to insist that there was absolutely nothing new about our vision. The model of Saint Hilda's House and Ascension House in New Haven, Connecticut, inspired us. We were moved by the rich Anglo-Catholic heritage of the parish out of which these initiatives have grown: Christ Church, New Haven, which proclaimed with equal boldness and humor a commitment to "worship like it's 1099": "We're not your grandmother's church. . . . We're your great, great, great-grandmother's Church." We were inspired by the Catholic Worker movement, with what Peter Maurin called "a philosophy so old it *looks* new."

The Community of the Franciscan Way's two Houses of Hospitality (Peter Maurin House and St. Elizabeth House) offer any in need or trouble a place of respite: a roof for wearied heads, a meal for empty bellies. It is a practice as old as Christianity itself. And older still. It's as old as Judas (not *that* Judas, but another) welcoming Saul-turned-Paul into his home (Acts 9:11). It's as old as the parabolic Samaritan who befriended a beaten-up traveler (Luke 10:25–37). It's as old as the Levitical admonition: "When an alien resides with you in your land, you shall not oppress the alien. The alien who resides with you shall be to you as the citizen among you; you shall love the alien as yourself, for you were aliens in the land of Egypt: I am the Lord your God" (Leviticus 19:33–34).

We've got a pearl of great price in The Episcopal Church. We've got that old tyme religion. We've got the wisdom of the ancients to guide us in the present, unto our future.

It is tempting to look out upon an aged and aging Episcopal Church and begin to scamper about, desperately scheming ways of attracting young people to keep up with the ultramodernevangelical Joneses (and in some respects, rightly so, as they're often doing really good things!). Faced with the ever-increasing numbers of agnostic, atheistic, or apathetic "nones," it's tempting to think that we've got to scrap the formula, bulldoze the edifice—as one emergent church put it, to "bake church completely from scratch." And while this may indeed be appealing to some, our aim in the Community of the Franciscan Way has been to lay claim to that which is distinctively (if not uniquely) ours: a philosophy so old that it *looks* new. Catholic Christianity. A deposit of faith that transcends the current fads and latest trends. Old tyme religion. Your great, great, great-grandmother's church.

What we've found is that lots of folks (young and not-so-young) are looking for Wrigley. They are looking for history, tradition. A wisdom of the ancients that can guide them through the morass of modernity. Many were raised on therapeutic, moral deism. They were spoon-fed a vapid, spiritless "form of religion that denies its power." They are looking for heft, for substance, for authenticity . . . for a people who are not trying to be something they are not but owning who (and whose) they are. They are looking for a people who know that they are claimed, a people who resist the pervasive myth that we have no story except the story we chose when we had no story.

Since the inception of the Community of the Franciscan Way, we've received e-mails and phone calls from (quite literally) all over the world. Young people ready to give up on whatever it is they are committed to and move across the country, desperate to join our way of life. They tell us that they see truth in the worship, discipleship, and way of life we're struggling to live. They see something real, demanding, costly. They see something worth

> They see something worth sacrificing for . . . and they seem ready to drop their nets and follow Francis as Francis followed Christ.

sacrificing for . . . and they seem ready to drop their nets and follow Francis as Francis followed Christ.

Tradition has been, for some, an awful—oppressive, exclusionary—thing. But it's time to take it back. It's time to assert a tradition that is radical; that is to say, getting back to the roots. Back to the roots of a story of a little poor man named Francis from Assisi, Italy. Back to the roots of a story of a Jew named Jesus from Nazareth. Back to the roots of a story of a liberating, redeeming, life-giving God. Back to the roots of a church bold enough to claim (as Christ Church, New Haven does): "Bread to body, wine to blood. . . . *That's* change we can believe in."

Reflection Questions

- *How do you practice authenticity?*
- *What is at the core of your faith?*
- *In what ways can the church rediscover what is essential and proclaim the Good News with integrity and authenticity?*
- *What is "the thing itself" to you?*
- *What does the word "tradition" evoke for you?*
- *What change do you believe in?*

CHAPTER THREE

Authenticity and Identity Crisis

Authenticity

Saint Hilda's itself might be an example of a church's authentic expression bearing fruit. The history and mission of Christ Church was bound up with the training of young men and women for ministry, in a disciplined life of prayer, in service to the wider community, and in regular sacramental worship. As we sought to develop some new mission effort, the congregation was invited to think about where they found joy as a community and how they could build on that. They might just as easily have been asked, "What is essential to your identity?" Our community grows out of this parish's understanding of its history, mission, and identity. It was not designed to rescue or fill a hole in our life together—it was built on what was authentically at the heart of the place already.

Perhaps a helpful place to begin, for Episcopalians, in a discussion of authenticity might be the baptismal covenant. As a Church, we have what we call a baptismal ecclesiology—our membership, leadership, and mission are formed at the font. As part of baptism we affirm the following:

Celebrant: Will you continue in the apostles' teaching and fellowship, in the breaking of bread, and in the prayers?
People: I will, with God's help.

Celebrant: Will you persevere in resisting evil, and, whenever you fall into sin, repent and return to the Lord?
People: I will, with God's help.

Celebrant: Will you proclaim by word and example the Good News of God in Christ?
People: I will, with God's help.

Celebrant: Will you seek and serve Christ in all persons, loving your neighbor as yourself?
People: I will, with God's help.

Celebrant: Will you strive for justice and peace among all people, and respect the dignity of every human being?
People: I will, with God's help.

The covenant outlines what it means to live as a Christian. We pledge to pray, participate in the Eucharistic feast, and study the teachings of the Church. We pledge to repent of our sins and return to God when we have fallen short. We pledge to be evangelists, missionaries, and agents of reconciliation. To be authentically Christian requires each of these in equal parts. As one visits various churches and seminaries, it is easy to hear one part or another of this Covenant stressed. Yet its parts interlock—they are tied together and mutually support one another and give form and spirit to the Christian life.

John Macquarrie writes of baptism, "Sin, or rather the conviction of sin, is the presupposition of baptism. We have a sense that all is not well with us."[5] The recognition of the weighing upon the Christian of the reality of sin impels us, calls us, to baptize our young and to be baptized ourselves in later life when so called. The baptismal mystery is that we understand ourselves to be washed from sin in baptism.

---

[5] John Macquarrie, *A Guide to the Sacraments*. (London: SCM Press, 1997), 68.

Yet we also recognize the reality of sin in our lived Christian experience. How do we hold onto that centered place in which we find ourselves at one with Christ, literally donning Christ at the font?

No sacrament can be studied in isolation from the rest of the Christian sacramental life. To do so is to impart a magical quality to the moments rather than framing them in the totality of belief, practice, life, death, hope, regret, grace, and pardon. Each sacrament must be taken as part of the whole of the experience of Christ's presence in and with us. Baptism, that moment of washing and donning, cannot be a moment but must be at once a beginning and end of the migration of lived Christian pilgrimage. Our entirety is baptized. Every aspect of our lives is knit to the divinity in baptism and we are provided a divine inheritance and calling. Humanity is invited to share in a destiny reflecting and foretelling divine grace.

Baptism is the sign by which we are to be seen, feel, and understand our life as awash in divine promise. As we are made one with Christ, we discover our true and authentic self. We might consider sin that which draws us from that authentic Christian life—away from who God has made us to be. Sin, washed from us at baptism, may still enter the Christian life and remove us from the awareness of the fullness of Christ's indwelling. Authenticity involves making the sometimes unobservable and the easily avoided more concrete so that we also feel the concrete reality of the grace of baptism.

Baptism encourages us to see others and ourselves as more than what is observable. We are invited to see the authentic amidst the false—amidst that which would separate us from one another and from God. The great gift of a sacramental worldview may be that of true sight. We become trained to see how God is truly calling the community, the individual, indeed all of creation to a deeper expression of its true Source. Just as bread and wine become body and blood—simple men and women are drawn into a yet more beautiful way. They are given a true self in the claiming of Christ.

We are moved, through the sacramental life, to a place where the outside, the observable, of others and ourselves is not its definition. For such an exterior definition is surely too often perceived only in such a way as to be useful and therefore violable. We are called to a place of deep respect in which our view of our fellow men and women is suffused with an awareness of their fundamental mystery, their belovedness as an inheritor of God's redeeming love. Their authentic identity and ours are bound up in the ceaseless love of God in Christ.

Sadly, our human perceptions have become the measure by which we map reality. Even more depressing, we have too often chosen usefulness or efficiency as our benchmark for deciding what is true or right or just. Yet can God have less use for a concept than usefulness? How often were flawed men and women the vehicles of his mercy and forgiveness? How often do we see God acting through the least likely to make his will known?

God is not calling us to think in terms of usefulness or efficiency—he is calling is to live authentically. This means being at once fairly ruthless in our honesty about ourselves and full of grace and mercy when we and others fall short. The baptismal covenant teaches us how a flawed "I" can be part of a blessed "we." In much of our seeking (our searching for who we are), however, we position ourselves out of false perceptions as to where and who we are in relation to the world around us rather than who we are in relation to Christ.

The baptismal covenant demands that we ask difficult questions about our life as individuals and as the Church as we seek to dwell ever more fully in the light of Christ. How are we, as individuals and as the Church, praying together? How are we evangelizing? How are we serving as missionaries? How are we repenting and returning to God? These are questions we need to be asking in an ongoing way, with an open and confessing heart, and with intention toward amendment of life where we are falling short.

There is a powerful link between a Church that is living into its corporate identity with authenticity and a Church that can draw young adults into its common life. One of the most powerful draws, for the young adults I work with, is a sense that a church is living an authentic life of service, worship, and prayer. This does not mean that every church looks the same—but that there is a core to its identity that comes across in different ways. For the Episcopal Church, this identity is expressed in our common worship.

Authenticity is a difficult thing to pin down. For example, I serve in a church from a particular tradition, the Anglo-Catholic tradition. I self identify as a relatively high church Anglican. Yet I have found myself totally at home in parishes that were Morning Prayer parishes, that were gospel parishes, that were Afro-Caribbean, and more. The common denominator was that each community felt like it was worshiping in a way that was utterly without pretense—their life was authentic. My greatest frustration comes when I visit places that are trying on things that are utterly foreign to their common life. For example, I visited a small church that was playing a recording of some grand hymn from King's College as part of its liturgy. The worship had ceased being the work of that community and felt utterly devoid of any sense of connection to their true life together.

One of the questions all churches must wrestle with is what its core identity is. Who are we and what do we proclaim? At the root of our identity must be the adoration of God. A worshipful Church that focuses its being on the adoration and proclamation of God in all things is one that can find the strength to stand fast—to dwell in the heart of God—when

> At the root of our identity must be the adoration of God.

challenges arise. A rooted Church can find the inspiration to serve, the joy to evangelize, the courage to speak for justice, and the daring to change its own structures.

There are concert halls that will offer more beautiful music. There are social service agencies that will serve the poor better. There are local community groups that will organize friends and neighbors more effectively. There are political committees that will lobby with greater impact. If our ultimate reason for being Church, for coming together, is not to worship God in his temple, then we should pack up and let professionals in these other fields handle the work. I believe there is a reason that the baptismal covenant begins with the breaking of the bread and the prayers. They are at the heart of our being together and fuel us for the rest of the work of the Christian life.

All of the other things the Church can do, the missions it can undertake, the ways it can be present in the community—all of those things flow out of a worshipful centeredness that must be planted deep in the heart of God. There is a definite link between authenticity as a community and the authenticity of its individual members. The Church that worships and serves with an authentic heart—a true heart—will encourage her members to live similarly grounded and true lives. Its rootedness will give them a place to grow and to flourish.

Benediction

At the heart of Christ Church's mission is the firmness of our identity as a place of adoration. This community knows who it is and what it believes. In a hypermarketed, oversold, and deeply cynical age, there is a need for the Church to offer a place of real and deep authenticity rooted in the worship of the Almighty. When people come in, they won't know everything that is happening, it won't be "relevant," and it won't be immediately decipherable. But it is deeply and powerfully authentic. Every movement and gesture kinetically expresses some bit of our faith. It is inherently and vitally real.

We offer, with regularity, stations of the cross and Benediction of the Blessed Sacrament. This act of walking and adoration is a powerful way to enter the story of Christ's passion. We journey through fourteen stations hearing readings and saying prayers that draw us in such that Christ's story becomes ours—even as we face the awful reality that we are also by sin complicit in his crucifixion. It reveals in many ways the essential quality of the Christian life—that even as we lay the cross on Jesus, he lifts its curse from us. Completing stations is an act of adoration of his presence in the sacrament. This serves as a kind of final station—the station of the resurrection. We adore Christ ever-present in our midst and made known more particularly in that vital and life-giving way.

A Jewish man once, having attended Benediction at Christ Church, asked, "So what just happened here?" He was at once perplexed but drawn in and saw that we were engaging some holy reality about which he wanted to hear more.

There are the objective measures of what happened. Jesus, made known in the sacrament, is before his people on the altar for them to offer adoration and praise and so that they may receive blessing and assurance from his presence. He is present in a way that demands little of us in the way that receiving in the Mass does—we are simply giving thanks and praise for the One coming among us in this particular way.

Benediction is a chance to offer that praise and to simply be in the presence of Christ. In a culture of too much noise and too little contemplation, we are given a space to be. Created elements, consecrated by divine mercy, are held aloft by sinful hands to be adored by loving hearts as the body sees and knows its source and fulfillment. Our hope is held before us, the ultimate sign of hope is made over us, and we lift our eyes and hearts in reverent thanks. In the Divine Praises, often said during Benediction, we hear and repeat the mystery of faith—that God dwells with us, is ever blessing us, and will make glorious that which often feels so feeble.

This part of our worship life is authentic. It is not exactly an easy service to get a handle on—to know "what just happened here." It invites inquiry, contemplation, investigation, and more in its very mystery. When those unfamiliar with the rite come, there will be questions. There will also very often be yearning to know more and hear who we are and who we worship. This encounter with an authentic expression of faith demands a response. We come not to be the person we were when we walked through the door—we come to be transformed, little by little, cup by cup, taste by taste, into him that we receive. We come to be transformed into the Body of Christ.

I offer this example (and the example of Saint Hilda's) as a way to think about ways your own community might have to offer an authentic expression of who you are as worshipers of Christ. How are you being called to more authentically participate in the prayers and the breaking of bread? Our experience has been that living into our uniqueness has drawn young people to us, rather than driving them elsewhere in confusion. There is some rootedness here that they find not only comforting but also compelling—that is calling them to live more deeply into their call as baptized members of the body.

Integrity—*Bob Griffith*

Before entering seminary, I spent many years at Kent State University as a campus pastor, graduate student, and then as an instructor and administrator. The experiences during those years were invaluable as I seek to understand how best to be present with the rising generations for the sake of the gospel of Jesus Christ and the cure and care of their souls. When I finally, but reluctantly, agreed to enter discernment for the priesthood, I made the vow to myself before God that through the coming years I would strive to be as vulnerable and genuine as possible. I knew that the students and younger people I worked with placed a high value on these virtues—they are seeking living examples of such things. It is not an easy task.

I am persuaded that the major consideration the Church needs to give attention to in these days is how we live out our lives individually and collectively within the greater society and within the institutions of the Church. Current culture experienced by the two most recent generations of Americans born since the early 1980s is now within the "Post-Constantinian Era" of Western Christianity and American society. Which means that the common culture no longer supports or even envisions an understanding of humanity, the world, and how we conceive of it all from the Judeo-Christian narrative and worldview.

Most members of these rising generations have not been raised with any kind of formal Christian education or exposure to parish life. Given this, our entire approach to spreading the gospel of Jesus Christ takes on a whole different patina and approach. We must consider issues around their self-described search for an authentic spirituality, which they convey as transparent lives that demonstrate a real, consequential experience of the Divine.

Most members of these rising generations have not been raised with any kind of formal Christian education or exposure to parish life.

What is the visible reality we as Christians maintain in the world as representatives of Christ's Church? Are we authentic to the enduring life in Christ or are we merely playing out an imagined rote script?

Our consumerist culture now compels us, as individuals and even as parishes, to project a mere image, a self-created avatar, an idealized persona that we use to try to convince everyone else we are who and what we want to be. Transparency demands that we admit what we are right now, even if not yet what we hope to be. We hear often from Millennials (born between the early 1980s through the early 2000s) that American Christianity simply regurgitates political agendas and is not particularly like Jesus.

In these times, for the Church to be authentic within Christ's invitation given to all people means that we have not given ourselves over to sociopolitical ideologies of the left or right. We must steer clear of convenience that compels us to avoid the hard and enduring proclamations of the Christian faith and religion. Church attempts at marketing are easily exposed, especially by savvy younger people who are bombarded with such things from birth. Where is the real, the authentic?

Truthfully, the hypocrisy and superficiality I witnessed and experienced among many of those claiming the name "Christian" within the institutions of American Christianity nearly drove me from the Church. I wasn't seeking perfection, but something with integrity, something authentic . . . something demonstrably real experienced by people that changed their very lives in significant ways.

A long-time campus pastor at Kent State who was coming to the end of his very successful career complained to me one day in the mid-1990s that his attempts to engage students suddenly took a sharp turn, and he was perplexed. He explained that he used to go on campus and easily get into conversations or arguments about God, Christianity, all of it. There was hardly ever a disinterested person unwilling to give him an opinion, whether positive or negative. Then somewhere in the 1990s, everything changed. Suddenly, it seemed, no one cared to talk. No one seemed to think that religion or Christianity had any real significance in life, so what was the point? Rather than an argument, there was a shrugging of the shoulders and a big figurative yawn.

In the 1990s, Generation X (born between the early 1960s through the early 1980s) and postmodernism were in full force on America's college campuses. A noticeable change developed in the common perceptions and experiences of college students in how they related to peers, their parents, authority, institutions, religion, and their understandings of life and the world around them. These fundamental changes were the logical result of earlier cultural developments coming out of the 1960s and can be traced up to the current crisis of authenticity.

During the decade of the 1960s, there was a decisive and collective generational decision to reject the personal, social, and religious experiences of earlier generations. The cycle that existed for millennia where the rising generation received elder wisdom and tradition, experienced them anew, and then passed them on to the next generation suddenly came to a generalized end. There was a determination to remake the world by way of a revised utopian vision of an imagined "Age of Aquarius." It was to be a brave, new world. This attitude worked its way into just about every aspect of generational thinking and approach to life. "Don't trust anyone over thirty"[6] was one of the mantras of the decade. The over-thirtiess, after all, were tainted by old-fashioned and outmoded thinking.

The interesting thing about this generation that rejected the convention and wisdom of past generations, however, was that they were already formed by it. Even while rejecting such things, the foundation had already been established, and thus their ability to reject it or accept it. What happened with the next generation, Generation X?

How often have we heard parents of the 1960s generational thinking saying something like, "I'm not raising my kids with any religion so that when they get older they can make their own decisions?" Well, as someone who received their kids as freshmen, I know that when those new students arrived on campus they had no idea how to even begin to judge a legitimate religious expression or organization from what might be a cult.

When members of Generation X began coming into their own, there developed a sense of being untethered from not much of anything other than peers. "Latch-key" kids grew up on their own, for the most part, with only TV and radio to take up much of their unsupervised time.[7] Without meaning being drawn any longer from enduring and tried sources, this generation began to draw meaning from popular culture. They were increasingly subjected to the crass and manipulative forces of marketing and hype posing as something of value and substance.

Does anyone remember "rich Corinthian leather"? It was presented as something chic, desirable, and a must-have for any up-and-coming anybody, even though there was no such thing as "Corinthian leather."[8] It is a fake. X'ers began asking, "What is trustworthy?" "What is real? A crisis of authenticity began to develop that continues to have far-reaching implications.

For Millennials, the situation has only been compounded with

---

6 See the YouTube clip of the "renewal" scene of the popular 1970s movie *Logan's Run*, depicting our future society that "renews" everyone when they reach their thirtieth birthday: http://youtu.be/LSUAAKFLoL0.

7 The hallmark movie of the generation can well be considered *The Breakfast Club* in all its angst.

8 From Wikipedia's entry for "Corinthian Leather," http://en.wikipedia.org/wiki/Corinthian_leather; and see Ricardo Montalban advertising the "luxury" of Chrysler's 1988 New Yorker: http://youtu.be/E_HMIN0nGl0.

very little residual remnant of elder wisdom or convention remaining. The result is that ethics became individualistic. The highest common moral value is to be nice. Subjective reality replaced objective reality. The tyranny of the immediate and superficial replaced the steady and significant. There is a real sense of abandonment by adults.[9]

When children are raised with little or no religious education and experience, the void will be filled. Into this void developed a new default "faith" described by the authors of the National Study of Youth and Religion[10] as "Moralistic Therapeutic Deism," which is not a Christian expression. The Internet and digital social networks have opened the world to younger people like nothing in human history. Yet we hear many adolescents asking how long they have to keep up their Facebook personas. They are worn-out trying to maintain the image of themselves that they believe will help them to be popular, accepted, and valued. They are telling us they need space to simply be themselves. For many, so wrapped up in it all, they need help understanding how to simply . . . be.

Several years ago while still in seminary, I did a summer internship in a Manhattan parish close to New York University. They had just resurrected the Episcopal campus ministry at NYU. One day I came into the office for a staff meeting and Father Andrew, the rector, just kept shaking his head and saying, "I just don't get it. I just don't get it." Finally, I asked him what he didn't get. He said, "One of our students, a young lady at NYU, said to me earlier today, 'But Father, we LIKE Rite I.' I just don't get it." When we consider the lives of our young adults and how to be present with them with the gospel of Jesus Christ, we have to have ears that truly hear and eyes that truly see whether or not what we witness aligns with our understanding of things. If we can do just that, and understand the enduring nature of our Anglican tradition, we will have authentic ministry.

Since rejection of past cultural wisdom and convention became the mainstay of education, entertainment, and even American Christianity, members of the emerging generations coming of age

---

9 See Dr. Chap Clark's books, *Hurt: Inside the World of Today's Teenagers* (Grand Rapids: Baker Academic, 2004) and the updated *Hurt 2.0: Inside the World of Today's Teenages* (Grand Rapids: Baker Academic, 2011).

10 See website http://www.youthandreligion.org/ (last accessed March 21, 2013).

over the past twenty plus years have collectively lacked a firm foundation upon which to base life, social interaction, and spiritual expression. Relationships and life in general were being navigated by X'ers without a guiding chart. Particularly among the Millennial generation, there is a rediscovery of that which is tried, tested, and honed over time. Authenticity is seen within enduring and traditional architecture, liturgies, language, forms of formation, and hymnody. With respect to the Church, there is an appreciation for confident proclamation of who we are and what we believe that still allows for wrestling with the faith.

If there is one thing Christ promises us, it is to know our true selves as we die to our old selves. In the transformative process as we yield ourselves to the Holy Spirit, we are re-formed out of the acquired cultural influences that work contrary to Jesus's example of a transparent and authentic life. According to their own words, such lives are a strong force drawing younger people into Christian faith and parish life. They are seeking transparent people who love God completely and love their neighbors sincerely.

Identity—*Ed Watson*

Authenticity is less a matter of what we do than a matter of who we are. It cannot be divorced from knowledge of self: if we are to be true to ourselves, we must know to which self we must be true. It is difficult to live an authentic life when trapped in the middle of an identity crisis, for Christians as much as anyone.

If we are to live authentic lives, we must figure out who we want to be, then figure out how to live lives true to this desire. Who we want to be is a question both of what we are and what we should be: to want to be someone who is necessarily beyond our grasp leads to self- destruction. (I will never be an Olympic sprinter, and if I were to set all my sights on trying to beat Usain Bolt, I would waste what talents I do have.) But to say we should be nothing other than what we are is to invite complacency. (If I am at present naturally selfish, I should work to change this.) What we want to be and what we are will depend in part of who we have been (we are all conditioned by our pasts), but it does not follow from the fact that we were once this way that this is the way we always should be.

What should Christians want to be? We are human; we cannot be perfect (or, if we can, then it would be solely through the grace of God). We can, however, strive for perfection in the full knowledge that we will, to greater and lesser extents, fail. What is perfection? A Christian life follows from the life and teachings of Jesus Christ, and Christian perfection is measured against these standards. Who was Jesus Christ? He was the Son of God; he embodied love fully through his self-sacrifice and death and the service of his life. He forgave, even though he alone was qualified to judge: he died, even though he alone deserved to live. He fed the hungry and he told us to do the same. He told us to love and serve the Lord; he did the same. Christians should want to be people who try their best to meet his standard.

Who have we been? Over history we've fallen short. This has sometimes been because of our humanity, sometimes because we've lost sight of who we should be. Christianity has often been a force for immense good. No matter what we may think of certain people's beliefs in relation to what we often call progressive values, there is little denying that they have done good work. Christianity has also exemplified the sin Christ warned against. The Church was not just complicit in but was one of the driving forces behind the racial subjugation of entire peoples; it has placed supreme importance upon its own traditions by confusing them for doctrine, and so made void the word of God. The fact that the most contentious issues in many churches at the moment are the ordination of women and homosexual marriage shows how far our vision has strayed. There is a very simple question to ask, "Would the ordination of women bishops hamper our ability to be what we want to be, both as individuals and as a Church?" Insofar as we are trying to live lives of more or less perfect servitude, the answer is no. The fact that these are thought to be questions of the identity of the Church shows how far many of us have misunderstood the question of Christian authenticity.

To be an authentic Christian is to try and live in accordance with the commands and teachings of Christ.

To be an authentic Christian is to try and live in accordance with the commands and teachings of Christ. These can be found in scripture, and in many cases (contrary to public opinion), they are relatively unambiguous: do not judge, love your neighbor as yourself, don't worry about stuff, etc. They are not always fluffy; "let the dead bury their own dead" is not a reassuring thing to read. But then, we aren't Christians for the sake of our own conventional comfort.

Sometimes being authentic means worshipping a particular way. Worship and prayer are, I think, essential components of Christian life: they focus our sight on God, and it is through this focus that we hope to better understand what we are called to do. How best to do this will depend in part on context, but for many of us (*including many of us who are young*) this means following certain liturgical traditions. By being part of a two-thousand-year-old tradition that allowed others to focus their sights on God, we can find ourselves directed toward Christ.

For some this does not work, but this isn't necessarily a problem. Authentic Christian worship must lead us to live authentic Christian lives, and different people will require different forms. What we must not allow ourselves to do is to miss the point of worship. Its purpose is not to engage for the sake of engagement, so we must not sacrifice everything for the sake of relevance. If being relevant means being inauthentic, then we must resign ourselves to irrelevance. The flip side is that by being inauthentic, we make ourselves irrelevant, so the dichotomy between authenticity and relevance is a false one. If we are not true to ourselves, how can we expect our truth to matter to the world?

Everything must relate to how we allow God to govern our lives and transform our beings. This is what we must focus on. Being authentic does not mean condemning homosexuality because it is what we've always done; it means feeding the hungry because this is what we've been told to do. It does not mean condemning sin because we have tried to take responsibility for humankind's salvation out of Christ's hands and place it in our own; it means living lives of love and service toward God and neighbor. It does not mean worshipping a certain way because it is what old folks think young folks think is "relevant" *or* choosing Rite 1 *because* this is how we've always done it; it means choosing Rite 1 because it focuses our minds toward God and living Christian lives.

Christians and the Church find their identity in Christ. To be authentic, and so true to ourselves, we must be true to Christ.

Reflection Questions

- *What is essential to your identity?*

- *How do you hold onto that centered place where you are at one with Christ?*

- *How do you live out the baptismal covenant?*

- *When have you been in the presence of Christ?*

- *In what ways does your community offer an authentic expression of worshipping Christ?*

- *What should a Christian want to be?*

CHAPTER FOUR

Rigor

Rigor

ONE OF THE GREAT GIFTS of Anglicanism might be what I would call rigor. The young adults that come to Saint Hilda's or that visit Christ Church are often looking, in so many ways, for that gift for their lives. They are often burned out on being either corralled down a particular path not of their own choosing or burned out on trying to make choices when the parameters for doing so have been divorced from deeper and more essential criteria of self-measurement. Anglicanism offers a way of connecting our lives, work, and faith in some ways that are profound in their simplicity. A life of rigor in prayer, service, and community is not about acts of willpower or the strength to assert the firmness of our will, but of the willingness and the faith to surrender to the Holy Spirit.

We share in a rigorous approach to prayer, scripture, service, and relationships that demand of us our very best and offers young people in particular a way to frame the whole of their lives so that they are neither denied the benefit of free choice nor left without a sense of the grander pattern of which their lives are a part. A bit about our life here at Saint Hilda's might be illustrative.

Each day at Saint Hilda's begins with Morning Prayer together.

We begin the day with the simple entreaty, "Lord open thou our lips." We hear the Word shared in community, recite the canticles that have been said in that chapel since its building, offer prayers of intercession and thanksgiving, and ask for Our Lady to pray for us in our daily lives through the Angelus. This discipline forms the heart of our community's life together. It demands something of us, especially those who are not morning people, and begins our day with the community coming together to give thanks and praise for all our blessings. This disciplined approach to prayer forms the backbone for the rest of the community life and shapes how we not only begin our days but how we interact with and treat one another.

One of my great joys is to watch and listen over the year as the psalms are recited together. In the monastic way, we read the psalms antiphonally from side to side in the chapel while pausing at the asterisk. At the beginning of the year, there are discordant voices. Some, too loud—some, too quiet. Some, too fast—some, too slow. Some rush the pause and others forget when it is their turn. Yet over the course of the year a rhythm emerges. The whole group becomes attuned to listening for breaths, to pausing, to either speaking up or quieting down. Eventually, they come to say the psalms with one voice, with one pattern, perhaps even with one heart.

This pattern is often mirrored in their common life together. Even as they strive to hear and listen for one another in prayers, in their daily life as a community, they reach that place where they are honestly listening to one another—waiting that extra beat before they speak. The intention of prayer becomes the intention of life.

The intention of prayer becomes the intention of life.

You can see this taking shape in our house meetings. At the beginning of the year, there is much energy devoted to saying "this is me" or "this is mine." As the year progresses and identities become more established, you begin to see them saying "this is us" instead. Mirrored in their life in the chapel is the evolution of their common life from the need to define the self in contrast to finding their voice in the deeper resonances of the community. Their passion, their energy, their drive comes to be shaped and informed by the needs of the community. This is profoundly countercultural. In a culture that celebrates the primacy of the individual, we are teaching them in prayer and relationship to seek first the well-being of the whole body of which they are a part.

Rigor in their prayer life becomes rigor in their common life. One might even think of rigor as deep intentionality—the conscious and ongoing attention to the pace and rhythm of life around them. One of our interns told me simply, "When I don't pray the Office, I don't feel like I am as good a person." He did not mean that he felt guilt for not saying the Office but that his mind and soul lost a bit of their connection to the will of God in his daily life. This connection, this ongoing guidance, this deeper sense of God's living Word being present are what young people are craving without necessarily being able to articulate it.

Part of our work at Saint Hilda's is simply to invite, through thoughtful and regular prayer, our interns to try on this way of mindfulness while they are with us. We do not necessarily think it is the only or the best way to make this daily connection to God, but it is the way we have inherited and share. We are bound by this common discipline to one another and to Christ. At the beginning of the year, many will grouse about the early time of day. Yet at the end of the year, when I ask them what the most meaningful part of the year was for them, almost all name regular Morning Prayer together.

The same discipline with which we approach Morning Prayer is reflected in other aspects of their common life as well. I began with prayer, but the whole of a week at Saint Hilda's is an experience of disciplined common prayer lived in multiple ways. Here is a brief description of a week here.

Once the interns have said Morning Prayer, they head off to work sites around the city to serve many who are most in need. Schools, soup kitchens, homeless shelters, and more benefit from their passion and energy. They work Monday through Thursday for thirty-two hours per week in those sites.

On Monday evenings, they have a regular house meeting with a house chaplain. At those meetings, they share what is going on in their lives and work to dialogue about the challenges and joys in their individual and common lives. This time also becomes a place to share pastoral concerns and to reflect on how they are living out their rule of life and their commitments to one another. Over the year, the group transitions from conversations that focus on the nuts and bolts of life together to broader topics of group and community dynamics such as personality types, group leadership, and more. Additionally, this space is sometimes used for participation in our social outreach ministries at Christ Church. We are blessed to have these groups facilitated by a fabulous chaplain who serves on the staff of Berkeley Divinity School at Yale.

On Wednesday evening, deepening our partnership with Berkeley Divinity School, the interns head over to the community Eucharist at Berkeley. This often provides a time for them to get to know a seminary community and the individuals there, many of who make their way to Christ Church. It is also a good spiritual recharge for those craving a more experimental worship experience.

On Fridays, we have a morning didactic discussion group. The curriculum I mentioned in the introduction is worked through in those discussion groups. As part of our common life, we commit to reading serious writings from patristic, medieval, modern, and contemporary writers on various aspects of faith. These tend to be serious works by authors such as Rowan Williams, Kenneth Leech, Miroslav Volf, John Macquarrie, and others. This is a critical piece of our program and, I believe, differentiates us from many other young adult communities. In addition to our regular reading, we also welcome a variety of guests, many of whom are leaders in their fields. The rigorous approach we take to engaging theology and society offers a grounded way for these young people to begin asking serious questions of their faith, their Church, and themselves.

On Friday, we share in a midday Mass together after which the interns head off for group spiritual direction. As with our house dynamics groups, we are blessed to have fine spiritual directors who share their wisdom and passion with our interns. This group offers a chance to simply dwell with God. It is often meditative in nature and balances out the rigors of didactic and house meetings. It is equally demanding in its own way but is designed to be a place of refueling and reinvigoration. For those for whom silence or stillness is a challenge, this group is especially valuable, as it provides a place to just be rather than to be doing more.

On Sundays, the interns are asked to come to one of our Sunday services. Many of them choose to become a fuller part of the worship by acolyting, ushering, reading, or helping with hospitality. We feel that no experience of the fullness of life together is complete without this time of worshiping together and being formed by the same worship experience. Like Morning Prayer, this is a touchstone piece of the program, as it offers a common language and frame for the rest of their week together. We also share in responsibility for setting up and taking down our Compline service and to offer hospitality for those attending.

In addition to this group life, we have also shaped their common life and space in such a way so as to reflect our commitment to the community. For example, interns have roommates (sometimes as many as two or three) but have a capacious common space. They have small individual stipends but rather more community money to share. Their space, time, budgets, time together, prayer, and more are structured so as to have the life of the community dictate the shape of the individual's life. In many ways, this is a foreign concept. Many find it challenging to balance the needs of the individual and community. Many struggle to find ways to healthily share or to be vulnerable. Many chafe at the regularity and structure of the schedule. This is a good and holy thing.

Holy Discomfort

Rarely does comfort produce spiritual growth. Our churches, and much of mainline Christianity, have struggled mightily to create churches that are nice, that demand little, and that have no visible bar, let alone a high one. Yet no such bland approach can change anyone, let alone change the world around us. It is only in learning to hear the voices of those around us, allowing those voices to speak to us, encourage us, and challenge us that we can grow as witnesses and disciples. In many ways, this kind of community is a laboratory for our engagement with the wider world. By creating a rigorous discipline for ourselves, we are training ourselves to be followers of Christ. These regular patterns of walking together enables us to more clearly and faithfully walk with Christ.

A faith that asks little and demands nothing is a faith that can't change anything.

> By creating a rigorous discipline for ourselves, we are training ourselves to be followers of Christ.

This life of rigor together binds us to one another in such a way that when one member suffers, all suffer and when one rejoices, all rejoice. The dangerous trend in faith and popular Christianity today is the quest for a comforting, affirming, benign, and banal God. The tidy popular spirituality being peddled these days offers little in the way of true, deep, and profound spirituality—it simply repackages our preferences and then lets us buy them back at a discount. Yet repackaged, plastic wrapped faith seldom leads to true joy. For it never asks us to die and be reborn. It never challenges us to eat flesh and blood and to have our feet washed. It never changes us.

The Episcopal Church in particular has gotten quite good at saying "Come as you are." Less often though do we follow up with "Leave transformed." A rigorous approach to faith offers a path for the transformation of the individual and the community.

The reverence we have for the life of prayer is a sign and indicator of the reverence we will have for other people—and for God's work through them and us. If we believe in our deepest heart that Christ is present and living in the world around us—and we seek to honor that presence with intentionality—then we can begin to understand Christ's presence in other people. The life of adoration and praise that is prayer demands of us that we adore those around us in the way God adores them. Not for who or what they appear to be but for who and what they are—the beloved of God. Not for what they can do for us but because of what Christ has done for us all.

A praying community is one that is forgiven and forgiving; a generous community that walks in the light and has fellowship one with another can never be a lazy community, for we are about the work of baptized living and transformed relationships. By that life together we draw others to the fullness of Christian living, as we know more concretely the emptiness of sin and the joy of forgiveness. We draw others to this life not because we think they are doomed otherwise but because we know where true joys are to be found. This is the true promise of a rigorous community of prayer—that it can become disciplined enough to seek first the will of God and strive for the good of his people.

Exhortations—*Neil Raman*

I recently had the experience of hearing the Exhortation from the Book of Common Prayer read aloud during a Sunday Eucharist. The Exhortation begins with a reminder of the mysteries and beauty of Christ's redeeming acts and the Eucharist. It goes on to call us to examine our "lives and conduct by the rule of God's commandments, that [we] may perceive wherein [we] have offended." To "acknowledge [our] sins before Almighty God" and to be "reconciled with one another" reminds us of the danger of receiving the sacrament unprepared. It is something that I had read when paging through the prayer book but had never before heard in the context of worship. It was a powerful experience, being called into an intense examination of self immediately after the corporate confession, and before the Great Thanksgiving and receiving Communion. It forced me to confront my walk and myself with Jesus in a new way. I don't, as a rule, like things like the Exhortation. I imagine this is true for most of us. People as a rule don't like being forced to examine their shortcomings. The Exhortation is jarring. It can come across as harsh. Indeed, it is harsh. It was so powerful for me because it was so harsh, because it was so uncomfortable. It made me sit up in my seat, take notice, and say, "Wait a second. This is new."

While I was sitting in that service, God, through the Church, was calling me into deeper accountability both with God and my community. I was being called, as the prayer book says, to judge myself, lest I be judged by the Lord.[II]

In the church we like to talk about transformational experiences. In our discussions, mission trips, days of service, and retreats are often mentioned, and for good reason; they often are transformative experiences, for through them we can learn to see God in Christ in new ways and in so doing deepen our faith. Many of these force us to confront the broken systems of the world and our complicity in them, or enable us to better understand the realities of God's love for us. Both are necessary things in the development of one's spiritual life; indeed it seems that I need reminders of both almost constantly.

[II] An Exhortation can be said before or at any time of the Holy Eucharist. One is found on p. 316 of the Book of Common Prayer.[AU: Please provide publication information.]

Also necessary are the things that cause us to look deep into ourselves and see ourselves as God sees us and change us in the ways that God is calling us to change. In my life some of these processes have started with guided retreats, but the ones that have been truly transformative in my life have been ongoing disciplines that need to be kept up with and maintained. These one-time experiences, while helpful, fade with time and the transformation that has occurred has the potential to fade over time like a foreign language being lost though disuse.

For me personally, taking on the discipline of praying the Daily Office has been incredibly fruitful. I began trying on this discipline while in college and for the next few years found myself going through short spurts of praying the Office each day followed by months of not doing so at all.

During my time at Saint Hilda's House, this discipline began shaping my life in real and profound ways. It became a matter of habit that at 8:00 a.m. each weekday I would be with the community in the Lady Chapel giving thanks to God, praying the psalms, hearing scripture, and petitioning God both on my own behalf and those of others. Some mornings I was attentive and engaged; other mornings the words just came out of my mouth out of habit. There have been times where I barely remember being there at all and the only way I know I've been is that I have to walk back to the house afterward. But it doesn't matter; it was prayer all the same. At some deep level, in the doldrums of my brain, the words of the psalms, canticles, and collects began to sink in and change the way I see the world. This practice began changing who I am and how I interact with the world.

> Beginning each day in prayer colors the rest of my interactions during the day.

Beginning each day in prayer colors the rest of my interactions during the day. It sets my mind on God in the morning so that I might be more open to his presence in the world around me throughout my day.

It is not at all that the Office is the best way of praying. The advantage of the Daily Office is that it gives a framework through which prayer, of some form or another can occur regardless of whether I am feeling "prayerful" or not. It doesn't matter if I'm not in the mood to pray. It doesn't even matter if I mean what I am saying. I can still pray the Office, and if I am not "feeling it," the very act of showing up and saying the words is in and of itself a form of prayer. It allows even someone like me, as weak and undisciplined as I am, to endeavor to pray daily and have a hope of succeeding.

This practice of daily prayer, these words that I pray, or on some days say only out of habit, has for me enabled the beginning of a transformation, that conversion of life that Jesus calls us into when he calls us to himself. It is a process that is wonderfully rich, but it is also a process that has a steep learning curve. The Daily Office was not something that I just stumbled upon; people I trusted in my church community recommended it to me. They invited me into a process of deepening my relationship with both God and community and served as comfort and support along the way. They asked me to try something difficult and for that I will be forever grateful.

All of this is to say that I want a church that expects things of me because it is the only way I am going to change. I want a church that is willing to say, "Each and every one of us is a sinner and just as we are all sinners we are all capable of continual conversion of life." Just as a rigorous academic program will change the way you think, rigorous expectations on prayer will change the way you live in the world. There needs to be the expectation of involvement and intentionality. The church should behave in a manner and ask in a manner that conveys the seriousness of what it is we are doing as the Body of Christ.

Christianity is not supposed to be easy, even if I sometimes want it to be. I want my church to comfort me when appropriate. But false comfort will not help me in the least. True comfort will be a help in my affliction while simultaneously drawing me into deeper relationship with God in Christ. I want the Church to ask hard things of me just as Jesus asks hard things of each of us who follows him. It is through the hard things that true change and conversion of life can take place. And if the Church does not ask us to do those things that are difficult, if we are not called into a deeper, a more disciplined relationship of discipleship with Jesus, how will we be able to do those hard things that Jesus will ask of us?

Ministry—*David Burman*

This year, I joined the acolyte corps at Christ Church. This entails a fairly large commitment. There are up to ten different acolyte roles in the Solemn High Mass as conducted in Christ Church, and each of them must be learned prior to actually doing them in the Mass. That means mastering different postures and movements, learning to watch other acolytes in order to know when to move, and remembering specific sequences of movement as they occur at different sections of the Mass. All of this is laid out in a document called the Customary, complete with specific directions and intricate diagrams, somewhat similar to an NFL playbook.

To a first-time acolyte, all of these directions and specifications and sequences have at times been somewhat difficult to learn, but knowing what to do when something inevitably goes wrong has surprisingly been the most rewarding part of being an acolyte. In the twenty or so High Masses at which I have served, there have been several occasions when I have either had little idea of what I was supposed to do next, made a mistake myself, or seen one of my fellow acolytes make a mistake. In unexpected situations like these, I tend to do one of the following:

hesitate, or

act extremely quickly and in something of a panic.

Yet what I have been slowly but surely learning is there is a certain pace to acolyting that finds a happy medium between these two extremes of inaction and rapid action, a pace that is especially important to maintain when something goes a little wrong. By remaining calm and continuing to move at a measured yet deliberate speed, the service can continue, and the mistake is quickly forgotten.

This pace that blends decisiveness with patience serves as a reminder that acolyting really is not about making each individual movement as correct as possible, but about manifesting Christ's presence to all the people present in the church through a careful attention to how we move. That this attention is perhaps most effective when something goes wrong is a reminder that God's grace is imminently present with us acolytes. "God loves you when you mess up," our acolyte coordinator has told us, and when I am able to overcome a small mistake by maintaining a worshipful pace of movement, I am especially aware of that love. It is the intention that is important.

I have found that the intentional pace that has helped me as an acolyte is also present within the community of eleven young adults of which I am a part. Right from the start of the program year with Saint Hilda's House, it was made clear that we are supposed to be more than just a group of people who happen to live together. In our first week we were assigned Dietrich Bonhoeffer's book *Life Together* (New York: Harper & Row, 1954), a short treatise which argues that living in Christian community is a fairly rigorous activity. Thus, we had hardly been together five days before we started reading about how we were supposed to bear one another's burdens, listen to each other, refrain from speaking ill of each other, pray together, pray *for* each other, worship together, read scripture together, and to do housework together, among other tasks. Unsurprisingly, the task of living in Christian community as presented by Bonhoeffer can be overwhelming at times, such as described in *The Cost of Discipleship*. Plus, he seems to stare demandingly out through his glasses at you in photographs.

But for Bonhoeffer, all of these tasks that are incumbent upon those living in Christian community are more than just duties to be fulfilled or not; they are "ministries," a word I am coming more and more to associate with grace. Far from being merely burdensome obligations, the ministries of living in Christian community are tasks to be approached with an attention and care that is inspired by God's grace, out of which great joy can emerge.

Having now lived in the Saint Hilda's community for about seven months, I have seen a few of the ministries described by Bonhoeffer acted out by us, with amazing results. There is the "ministry of listening," which for Bonhoeffer means a wholesale attention to the words of another, and not a sort of half-listening that is distinguished by the presumption of already knowing what the other person

> I have found that we are at our best when we take the time to listen to each other.

is trying to say.[12] While we are far from perfect at carrying out this particular ministry, I have found that we are at our best when we

---

[12] Bonhoeffer, *Life Together*, 97–99.

take the time to listen to each other. Lately one of the most important venues for listening to one another has been found in our prayer partner system that we Hildans created, in which we pair off each week with another Hildan and pray especially for that Hildan. Early in the week, I have usually met up with my prayer partner so that we can both get a sense of what the other person would like for us to pray about. These meetings have been marked by a sort of holy listening that seems to free me from my own concerns to hear what is going on in my prayer partner's life, and to pray for that person.

I have also seen the "ministry of helpfulness" acted out in our community. By "helpfulness," Bonhoeffer means a spirit of service to others, especially when we don't plan to give service. We like to live our lives according to a preset plan, Bonhoeffer argues, and so we are surprised and often annoyed that our life is "crossed and balked" by the unexpected needs and concerns of others. But when we realize that God often calls us to service in these unexpected moments, then the community is built up.[13] This year we Hildans have interrupted our routines to visit each other in hospitals, help each other finish up chores, or even attend a concert at which one of our housemates was performing. This spirit of giving service or even presence may seem unimportant at first within the context of our day-to-day lives, but over time it has welded us closer together as a community.

Imperfect as they are, our efforts to minister to one another in these ways and in others has provided for me a glimpse of the sort of community Bonhoeffer describes when he writes about what happens to someone who undertakes the ministries of community:

> Now he can allow the brother to exist as a completely free person, as God made him to be. His view expands and, to his amazement, for the first time he sees, shining above his brethren, the richness of God's creative glory. . . . Now the other person, in the freedom with which he was created, becomes the occasion of joy, whereas before he was only a nuisance and an affliction.[14]

---

[13] Bonhoeffer, *Life Together*, 99–100
[14] Ibid., 93.

As with acolyting, Christian community living is not about how much or how often we "get it right" and successfully fulfill our obligations. It is instead about our intention, the care we take to serve and be present for one another, and to see the other as God made them to be, not as we would like them to be. We get it wrong over and over again of course, but it is in those moments especially that God fills us with grace, enabling us to enter into that intentional state of mind through which we can begin again the task of living together in community, just as a worshipful pace of movement enables me to overcome mistakes when I am an acolyte.

Reflection Questions

- *What do you practice with rigor in your life?*

- *How do you simply "dwell with God"?*

- *How do you balance your individual needs with those of any community or group that you belong to, including work and family?*

- *What does faith ask of you? What does faith demand of you?*

- *What does it feel like to be "confronted" by your shortcomings during prayer or worship?*

- *How do you manifest Christ's presence to others?*

CHAPTER FIVE

The Beauty of Holiness

Beauty

ANGLICANISM IS, PERHAPS, A FORM of Christian expression that is uniquely suited to poetic explorations in its famous indeterminacy. Its concern more for a way of being as opposed to specific and dogmatic proclamation has marked its history in unique ways and continues to influence its patterns of worship and overall ethos. Anglicanism, alike to poetry and spirituality, is fiercely articulate without being given to determinate definition and finds its richest expression in calling the individual into a deeper relationship with God and the world without prescribing or proscribing in a rigorously confessional sense. Beauty creates the space for meaning to be mediated as it takes on the role of sustained and holy metaphor through which we begin to see and know that which is unseen. This sustained metaphor is a link and mediator between our natural human instincts and yearnings and the teaching of tradition and the creeds.

When visitors enter Christ Church, the beauty of the place often strikes them. There is a powerful sense that the building is at prayer. The lingering smell of incense, the rays of light, the quiet punctuated by the sounds of the city, the bells tolling out the hour, the candles slowly burning down near the shrine—each of these speaks to the vocation of the place. It is a house of prayer. It is designed to communicate something of the divine-human encounter made known in the person of Christ. Through its beauty we come to an awareness of that which is fundamental to all even as it lies in a deeper beyond. Christ Church is precise as it is in its form (and its liturgical and prayer life), reflecting long tradition, but full of a sense of fresh engagement with the divine.

The building's beauty both teaches and invites. It teaches us, bit by bit, of the faith and invites us to a life of deeper prayer. When one simply walks from the font to the altar, it becomes a pilgrimage in its own right as you travel along a path marked by the virtues of the Christian life. Nearest the font, in brickwork on the floor, is the word *fides* or faith. Yet *fides* has at its heart trust, the beginning of the life of faith. The life of baptism is trust. Trust in God's promises and redeeming power. As one walks along the axis from the font to the altar, one walks a path of virtues loaded with meaning and promise for the Christian life—*virtus, sapientia, temperantia, patientia, bonitas, benignitas,* and finally *humanitas* (virtue and valor, wisdom and discernment, temperance and restraint, patience and endurance, goodness or excellence, kindness and benevolence, and human nature and civilization).

This walk culminates under the rood screen, with its powerful image of Christ reigning crucified, as if to say that the promise of the risen Christ is made known in the life of virtue—that by walking this path one arrives at the foot of the cross and moves to fulfillment in the risen life at the altar.

If one walks the interior paths along the stone walls, one walks the way of the cross. The stations of the cross invite the pilgrim, even for a moment, to stand along with Jesus on the Way. We find ourselves in various stations seeming to help carry his cross, or to help wipe his face, or even to help place him on the cross, and to lay him in the tomb. Each station makes the story come alive in such a way that we are welcomed to the memory and find our place in its unfolding all about us.

Something about this place of beauty—its authentic articulation of the classic faith—creates a place for young adults to find a

> *Something about this place of beauty—its authentic articulation of the classic faith—creates a place for young adults to find a home.*

home. In its timelessness they find a place to stand amidst the shifts and upheaval of many of their lives. It is a place of blessed assurance and it is a holy place because it communicates knowledge of God and offers a relationship with him. The whole of the place—its liturgies, its prayers, and its outreach—are designed to express the source of holiness, the fruits of the life of holiness, and the final promise of holiness.

This kind of beauty demands a response. It is not something that can be just looked upon—it asks us to behold. To behold the wonder of the hosts of heaven in the *Te Deum* window. To behold the offering poured out on the cross at the twelfth station. To behold the Blessed Mother's love at the Lady Shrine, to behold the patriarchs, prophets, and martyrs making bold their proclamation in the reredos (the wall behind the altar). We behold his glory in this place. From seeing deeper truth in everyday relationships all around us, to seeing by faith and grace the True Body and Blood in the Eucharist, to seeing the order of nature announcing the love of God, beholding is what separates the holy from the merely living.

In the day-to-day lives of many young adults, they will be assaulted by images of at best banality and at worst outright cruelty. Advertising works on the premise that they are never enough, television creates a spectacle of emotional manipulation and invites them to cascade between feeling less than or superior to—megastores and strip malls take nature and bend it to serve only a bland commerce in a landscape painted only in beige. All of the consumer culture is bent toward creating competitive identity that obscures our actual identity and blurs the particularities of the neighborhoods we live in and serve.

Somewhere along that walk from the font to the altar, in the life of virtue, the encroaching of cultural norms, values, and expectations derails us. The journey that we begin by being baptized into the life of Christ quickly gets sidetracked as we take paths that seem to shine a little more brightly. Then we find ourselves lost and without bearings—unable to see our true selves or true home through the ceaseless press and clamor.

The hollowness of the world cannot be filled with more of the world, but with more of that grace which flows of the sacraments and makes men and women more holy and more devout. Those struggling to find God amidst and despite the banality of much of contemporary culture will not find an answer in a Church that simply seeks to replicate that banality in our buildings, liturgies, prayers, or work in the world.

This is where beauty comes in. Beauty has the power to pull us up short—to force us to behold again. To behold all that God is doing around, in, and in spite of us. It demands of us a renewed seriousness as we stand in the middle of that which makes us know that there is more. One of our interns said that he appreciated our emphasis on sacred time—real life has rhythms like seasons and the individual Christian's life should too. The Christian life is a sacred thing that unfolds in the patterns of the Church year. Beauty calls us to stop and know the sacredness of a moment and a lifetime. It is a bridge by which people come to find God, for it changes the heart, points it toward the possibility of the universe, and prepares the mind to think in terms of mystery. Beauty offers a means by which the individual is given a greater depth of awareness over time so that they may no longer be superficial but may partake of the nature of the holy.

Beauty doesn't have to be the Gothic revival that is Christ Church. It is often found in the simplest and most mundane of things. In Chinese calligraphy, artists often spend years learning to master the simple straight line. Speed, intensity, nervousness, training, concentration, and more are communicated in a simple stroke that moves from left to right on a scroll. In that simple black line on white paper, a story unfolds that is elegant and potent in its starkness.

The kind of beauty the Christ Church embodies says something of our relationship to God. The best we have in music, fabric, woodwork, stonework, iron, poetry, movement, glass, and more are offered for the adoration of God. It is as lavish an offering as the oil used to anoint Jesus's feet. It is all that we have and expresses all that we hope to be—fully devoted to an unstinting outpouring of our thanks and praise.

Young adults are reengaging with a Church that they often know little about. They do not necessarily have doctrinal opinions; they have often not been formed in the patterns of liturgical life and time; they often only know this place holds something for them to come and see. We offer

We offer a place of rest and engagement that stimulates all of the senses and calls them to be still.

a place of rest and engagement that stimulates all of the senses and calls them to be still. We often get young people coming out of vaguely Roman Catholic or evangelical backgrounds who find in this place not a way of thinking but a way of being—a way of dwelling with Christ and finding God speaking through the numinous.

Transcendence

Beneath the exterior beauty of the place is something yet more profound. At its heart is an approach to thanksgiving and self-offering that is deeply authentic and articulate beyond words. The physical manifestation that is the building carries within its walls the rigorous approach to prayer and service that have marked this place through its history. The building expresses the heart of the people even as it continues to call and shape souls. It is in holy conversation with us and us with it. Our reverence made known in time and place calls us to a reverence for one another. It is only natural that intentional communities have developed over history in places like this because the life of intentional self-offering is made known across our common life and space in various ways.

Modernity, in its rush to be ever more "objective" and fact-based, has lost the conception of the beautiful, and with that loss has come the inability to know beauty as a means to understand the world around us. When we lose the concept of a "beautiful" outcome due to our need to be ever more objective, we subordinate the "subjectively" beautiful to the "objectively" factual. In doing so, we lose the ability to aspire to a world and a Church that is based on a mutuality of vision and shared story. Young adults are formed in a society that gives primacy to individual achievement rather than shared identity. So rather than being encouraged to seek the deeper beauty that is our common life in Christ, they are trained to simply succeed with achievement as both the means and the ends.

Meaning in such a system becomes one more outcome or product rather than the drive or the framework for the pursuit of human endeavor. For theology, the loss of beauty is the loss of our ultimate center as Christians. Christ is the form and beauty that defines our hope and us. Thus our churches, our liturgies, our service in the world, and more are given shape and meaning by the beauty we find in the life, death, and resurrection of Christ. As those sacred spaces, liturgies, and prayers ever more become a medium for us to talk more and more about ourselves and less and less about God, we will cheapen faith and create no compelling, authentic, beautiful identity that draws others into life together.

There cannot be a Christian conception of beauty without understanding the compelling and transcendent beauty of lives lived fully in the service of Christ and the whole of humanity. For beauty is necessarily transcendent, and fundamentally calls us out of ourselves into the world and history to greater service and purpose. Thus the Christian call is an aspect of beauty, for it reflects the ongoing transcendent love of Christ in the world and through his people in the site of redemption, Creation. This is a poetic encounter that understands revelation as a poetic act of compelling content. Part of that poetic encounter is the call of the cross. The very nature of the cross is the beauty that declares the politics of the world to be false. It is the triumph of the "antikingdom" or the unkingdom over the will of the state or of the individual.

By small acts of service and devotion we become more than symbols of God's love—we are drawn together as the Body to be a sign of the beauty of redemption. These acts are not about us, though. We are not a social service agency, political action committee, or a civic board. We do this because the love of Christ compels us. These simple acts are the means we have to be community—to live a sacramental life—a life that becomes an outward sign of God's grace.

The Church is both that which can be seen and "works" in the world. It is a body of people that can be seen and understood as answering human needs. The Church is also holy. It is mysterious and its purposes are not ours but God's as it changes the hearts of men and women. Its levers are held by humanity, but it is not under their control even as it does require their vibrant participation to keep it alive. The Church is an active, living, and changing body, yet forged in the depths of tradition. Beauty draws us into the work of God with awe—it is not deduction of or even emotional response to God that will ultimately lead one closer to him, but the more simple action of living by wonder in prayer.

The Beauty of Brokenness—*Sarah Raven*

When I first arrived at Christ Church, New Haven, the Gothic architecture and the amazing stained-glass windows in the church struck me. The elaborately carved wooden rood screen with an athletic Jesus on the cross is not only eye-catching, but also beautifully terrifying in its intricacy. Walking around the nave it is clear that every inch of the building was lovingly planned and shaped by master craftsmen—people who created a unique space with wood, metal, and glass that generations of families and individuals would call "home." As an outsider to Christ Church, it can at first seem cold and distant. The vacant stare of statues and icons, the ceiling that soars to the heavens . . . it is not the setting of a cozy house Mass. But when the lights come down and the candles are lit, as is customary for the evening Compline service, then the entire space is transformed to a warm breathtaking loveliness that is as mysterious as it is alluring.

At my first Compline service, the candles were ablaze all around the sanctuary, and I sat in nervous silence as the incense rose to the ceiling. Then voices of "angels" burst out into melodic harmonies and descants. Somewhere between the ancient hymns, the flickering candles at the altar, and the smoke from the frankincense dancing around the flames, I found a deep peace. Tears began to roll down my cheeks as I realized that this space for meditation and reflection was missing in my life. I reflected on the fact that most people do not have the privilege to take time out of their busy week for such beauty and wonder.

Tears began to roll down my cheeks as I realized that this space for meditation and reflection was missing in my life.

So I cried not only out of an overwhelming sense of joy and gratitude, but out of sadness for the people of New Haven who are unaware that in the midst of all the sirens and cacophony of the city, available to all is a few minutes of ethereal ecstasy. Instead of standing up and sitting down, and anticipating sacred invocations, I was actively engaged in another type of worship. I was a vessel being filled by song, by darkness, and by the still quiet voice of God found in smoke, in fire, in music, and in silence.

Several months later I was among a group of Saint Hilda's House interns who worked for hours at a time for several weeks trying to repaint, redecorate, and rebuild Ascension Church in the Hill. The building was clearly in need of love and care and stood in stark contrast to Christ Church. At Ascension the stained-glass windows were cracking and falling out. The plaster on the walls crumbling, the wood rotting. I looked around in distress and despair. The luster of this worship space had long faded, and it struck me that this was in some way a metaphor for my own life.

On my spiritual journey I have often felt a lack of polish and elegance. The bitterness and hurt that wells up inside when I am aware of my doubt is palpable. I struggle with believing in God and believing in myself. When people preach a sermon about God's love, or our overwhelming pulchritude in God's eyes, I am often left feeling numb or angry. "If God loves me, why does he allow me to suffer?" "Why is there so much ugliness and oppression in the world?" But the story of my faith journey runs parallel to the story of building and rebuilding our neighborhood church. It is a narrative that is incomplete without second chances and without grace.

When Father Robert Hendrickson reclaimed Ascension, and vowed to rebuild the sanctuary, simulating the splendor and warmth of Christ Church, it became apparent that even a once desolate place is worthy of love and redemption. People bound up in the story of Ascension, people like myself, are therefore also worthy of love and redemption in the eyes of God. I cannot prove that this is true, but standing in the freshly painted Ascension Church, marveling at Our Lady of Guadalupe in front of a backdrop of rod iron votive holders and an antique gold wall, I found some hope that God's grace is real.

I began to wonder more about material things, about buildings, stained glass, art. Is it possible that God's love and grace is made manifest through things that we see around us every day? Not just in animals, and in the love of other humans, but in material culture itself? Then I began to wonder about the material that we waste. If God is speaking to us through bread and wine, blood and flesh, is God also speaking through broken glass, through crumpled paper, and if so, what is God saying?

I once told God that I am a very hard-headed person and I need very concrete examples in order to follow God and to "hear God's voice." When I was discerning whether or not to go to seminary, I went on a jog around a park in Denver. I said to God, "If you want me to know what you want me to do, you're going to have to give me a sign. I don't mean one of those metaphorical signs either; I mean an actual sign or I'm not going to know it is from you. So what God? What do you want me to do with my life? Just tell me!!" At that moment I looked up and across the street from where I was jogging was a giant banner that was hanging on the side of a church that read simply, "Called to Serve." So I do believe that God uses concrete, brick, glass, metal, paper, and wood to guide us and teach us something about his desire for us and his kingdom.

Because I am called to serve and because I firmly believe God has called me to use materials around me to teach others about his mercy and love, I have started a green art program at Ascension called GARLiC (Green Art Recreating Life in Communities). In this program students will take art classes, learn how to reuse what they have, and "upcycle." Upcycling is essentially taking something that would have been thrown away and modifying it in some way to make it more beautiful. Upcycled things are usually products that have some practical purpose, but at GARLiC we also make art that serves no function other than to dazzle the eye with its winsome qualities.

In my life, God is the Lord of upcycling. He has rescued me from being thrown away by society, and from throwing my own life away—time and time again. God is constantly working with and through me, desperately trying to modify me for a higher purpose. Although I consistently undercut my own worth, God consistently acts as supreme appraiser and tells me that I have a greater value than I can ever imagine. But doubt creeps in and looking at myself, I rarely believe that I am worth anything at all. Perhaps in one of the greatest ironies, I have come to realize that this for me is the project; my vocation and calling is to try to convince other people who have been marginalized and "thrown away" of their intrinsic worth, and the redeeming work of God through art, craftsmanship, and beauty. The classes offered at GARLiC will engage people in discussions about being good stewards of the environment, reducing waste, recycling, and creating beautiful things out of things that were discarded or forgotten.

I don't have any illusions that doing this work will suddenly cure my doubt, or raise my self-esteem. However, I do know that there is something in a candlelit Compline service, in an ornate Gothic church, in a stained-glass window, in a painting, in a sculpture, or in a discarded bottle that simultaneously represents the incarnational savior and the transcendence of God. God is with us and God is bigger than we could ever fathom, and more beautiful than we would ever contemplate. God is the most exquisite work of art and the master craftsman and I am humbled to be his work in progress.

Being Found—*Erika Takacs*

In some ways, the story of my faith when I was a young adult is the story we're all taught to expect. A family that prayed, read scripture, and talked about our faith regularly raised me in the church. When I went to college, though, my faith was soon pushed to the very fringes of my life, and by the time I graduated, I wasn't attending church at all. After a few years, though, when I began to develop my life as an adult, I chose church again, opting for a different denomination than the one in which I had been formed as a child. When I was a child, I churched like a child, but when I became a woman, I gave up those ways for something more *me*.

That's the simplest, sparest version of events. But the real story is far more complicated, far more challenging, and far more wonderful. (I expect that's true for most of us, isn't it?) An extremely devout family raised me in the church, but the truth is that I was raised in an extremely devout family of Christian Scientists, which meant that church and prayer and scripture look far different than they do to most Christians. It also meant that my family and I chose not to use any form of medicine when we were ill; instead, we prayed to "get our healing," sometimes calling on the help of a paid Christian Science practitioner to help us accomplish that goal. I took the faith of my childhood very seriously. I loved going to church as a child (or Sunday school—children do not attend Sunday services at all in the Christian Science Church). I even chose to go on Wednesday nights sometimes with my mother, who served as a reader in the church and as such led these midweek services of prayer and testimony. When I started college, I participated in the campus group for Christian Scientists and continued to go to church with my family, who lived close enough to pick me up for Sunday services.

But very quickly into my college career, everything changed. My mother told me during the course of my freshman year that she had developed what she thought was breast cancer (having not gone to the doctor, she was guessing at the diagnosis) and was going to try to "get her healing" through Christian Science. She immediately hired a practitioner for help and began reading and studying and praying fervently, looking for physical signs of healing. They never came. By the next year, she was so weakened that she had to go into a Christian Science sanitorium (a kind of nursing home), and she died my junior year, following a desperate last-minute attempt to employ medical science to heal something that had long progressed past the point of any cure. When she gave up on Christian Science and went into the hospital, I turned my back on the religion of my childhood and never stepped into a Christian Science church again.

So in one very fell swoop, I lost my mother, my church, my faith, and my God. I was lost and angry and not at all interested in trying to reestablish some kind of contact with a religion that had let me down or with a God who seemingly had turned his back on me. But I did want my life to have meaning and truth, and so I began to look for that sense of purpose in other places. I found it in my then vocation, in the depth and beauty and transcendence of music.

I did want my life to have meaning and truth, and so I began to look for that sense of purpose in other places.

My undergraduate degree is in music education, and after a year of teaching in a public school as a long-term substitute, I began a master's program in choral conducting at Westminster Choir College in Princeton, New Jersey. Westminster has its foundations in the Presbyterian Church (Westminster Presbyterian Church in Dayton, Ohio, is where the choir that ultimately founded the college had its origins), but it has long ago lost any religious affiliation. So I did not find the Church there; what I did find was a community that honored and prized a certain way of music making and with it, a certain way of being in the world. My conducting professors spoke to me of honesty and truth, of being faithful to the music as it exists on the page (and perhaps in the ear of the composer), of breathing with an open heart and mind, of occupying both aural and physical space with the choir, *as* the choir, as one who serves to conduct the beauty of the transcendent moment to the world. This was profoundly moving—and profoundly spiritual—stuff. And it got me by; it helped me to endure this excruciating time in my life. Music made meaning for me, provided joy and moments of indescribable and unearned beauty, and I was happy.

Well, I was happy until I wasn't. Because eventually, after years of turning my face away from God with some force and with lots of self-defeating arguments about how I didn't believe that he actually existed (so he could stop trying to talk to me, thank you very much), I found myself searching for something—for something deeper, something else, something *Other*. I couldn't quite believe that this Other was truly God (after all, we hadn't made up yet), but I started searching nonetheless. Was it self-help I needed? A better therapist? Oprah Winfrey? I tried all of these things, and all of them actually helped . . . to a point. But the yearning was still there, and none of these things fully satisfied that longing.

As these things often do, it took a moment of crisis for me to realize what I was really missing. I was preparing for my graduate conducting recital—a time fraught with angst and self-doubt and stress by the boatloads—and I had had a particularly dismal rehearsal. I was crushed, convinced that this rehearsal proved something that I had suspected for a long time—that I was a fraud, that I had no business doing what I was doing, that I was talentless and a bother and an impediment to the making of true, beautiful music in the world. As you might imagine, I completely fell apart. My advisor and mentor took me to a quiet place in the basement performance library where we could sit (and I could cry) in relative peace. I asked him—sobbingly, if I remember—what I was supposed to do. What are you supposed to do when you can't make the music the way you want to? What are you supposed to do when your ears seem stopped up and your hands as heavy as lead? What do you do when you can't breathe, can't connect, and you feel like you're standing outside of yourself watching yourself fall apart? What then? I had no answer to this question and fully anticipated that there was, in fact, not one. So imagine my surprise when my professor looked up at me and said, quietly, "Well, it's at moments like that that I learn a lot about grace."

What?!? Grace?!? But we aren't talking about God here, we're talking about music, I thought. But then, just like that, the scales fell from my eyes and I realized what I had really been looking for. In my heart, I needed to find God. Again. Or to let myself be found. Again. And somehow, in that grace-filled, life-changing, lightbulb moment, I was ready for that to be the answer. Yes, of course. That's what I need. God.

Of course, I had no idea who God was or what he wanted with me, but at least I was willing to say hello. So at first, that's all I did. I would sit in the quadrangle of the school before rehearsals, listen to the wind in the trees, and say, "Hello, God. I have no idea who you are or what you want from me, but I would like to tell you that I'm happier with the idea of a world with you in it than the idea of a world without you in it. That is all. Love, Erika." And that was enough . . . until it wasn't. So soon I found myself church shopping, and although I wasn't exactly finding what I was looking for, the searching brought me great joy. Naming my longing, knowing what I was looking for, even when it hurt, helped.

Soon after graduation I was offered a job singing at Saint Mark's Church, Philadelphia, an urban, Anglo-Catholic parish that grounds its life in beauty—the beauty of worship and the beauty of serving the poor. Within weeks, I knew that this "church job" was much more than just a Sunday gig. Something was working within me. I can remember singing some profoundly beautiful setting of the *Kyrie eleison* of the Mass and suddenly realizing that I was actually praying, "Lord, have mercy." Or actually trying to, at least. And so I started engaging with this community of faith—I spoke to the priest, started in the catechumenate, was baptized and confirmed, and then slowly found myself taking the initial steps to begin the discernment process for Holy Orders. In a strange and wonderful and surprising twist of grace, I now find myself serving the parish that lifted me up as the associate rector, helping to expand the ministries of music and service here, offering my own gifts in this beautiful place to the greater glory of God.

What was my experience as a young adult in the church? Not so unusual really—it was the experience of being lost and then being found, of being blind, but now I see. But it wasn't *just* a friendly face or a sense of welcome that helped me to find my spiritual home; it was finding a community that takes beauty seriously, a church that understands the power of symbol without claiming to understand every facet of the symbols themselves. There is room for mystery here. There is room for Other, for bigness, for the Almighty who fills this holy temple with wall-to-wall garment. There is room for a sense of the Transcendent One who broods over the waters of our turbulent souls like a mother and then swoops down on her mighty wings to speak to us, as close as the lips of our neighbor, as close as our breath, as our own souls. I needed this kind of breadth and depth and height in my spiritual life; I needed space for the wideness of the beauty that I sought in my music and that I now also seek in prayer and worship and service. And I see this need in many of the young adults who now find their way to our door. They're looking for something Beautiful and Real and Other and Friend. And I am always happy to tell them my story—the story of a lost, frightened, and injured sheep, who heard a tune of such beauty being whistled in the wind that she turned around to look, only to find herself looking into the grinning, beautiful, familiar face of her Savior, arms spread wide, calling her home.

> *I needed space for the wideness of the beauty that I sought in my music and that I now also seek in prayer and worship and service.*

Reflection Questions

- *How do you respond to "beauty"?*
- *Where do you find beauty in the world around you?*
- *How can we put the search for beauty ahead of the search for success or achievement?*
- *When have you been filled with the still, quiet voice of God? Where were you? What were the circumstances?*
- *Do you believe that it is possible for God's love and grace to be manifested through things around us? Why or why not?*
- *When have you experienced God's grace?*

CHAPTER SIX

Catholicity

Pilgrims and Tradition

CATHOLICITY IS ONE OF THOSE terms that are easy to misunderstand and misapply. Its quickest connotation, in the popular mind, is the Roman Catholic Church. This is natural, yet it creates an unfortunate shorthand for a much broader word and concept. In working with young adults, one of the ideas they communicate in different ways is the desire to belong to something bigger than themselves. In a culture of shifting identity and marketed notions of self and belonging, they are yearning for something that is rooted, authentic, inviting, and transformative—this may be a helpful way to consider catholicity.

It is a concept that draws young adults because it is about the fullness of their lives and their identity and offers a vital and very real way of being the Church. In many ways, this helps them to create a "tribal" identity of sorts. As young adults look for a way to articulate who they are, these markers of the community's story become their own as they establish what makes them who they are at the deepest levels.

Young adults often strive to mark who they are by means of specific identifying markers—think of the various subgroups that develop in schools. The challenge is to help them find something that is deeper and of more lasting import that offers a distinctive sense of belonging and identification. In this way, catholicity offers a sense of home even as the journey is ongoing—an identity for a pilgrim tribe. Those churches that thrive seem to be those that offer some way of being distinctly and distinctively a part of the community in a way that changes the individual. Each community must have a story—a way of sharing who it is—that offers what I would call an enlivening welcome. This kind of welcome is the kind that stirs the heart to strive for more and to be a part of whatever distinctly sacred thing is happening in this time and place.

There are two vital words associated with Catholicism within Anglicanism. The first is Church and the other is communion. The Episcopal Church offers a way of being Church that is different in important ways from the way Protestant denominations order themselves. It is a Catholic Church that is sacramental, in apostolic succession, and preserves the ancient orders of ministry. A Church's call is broader than that of a denomination—its goal is not institutional maintenance but the welcoming of all into the way of Christ. It is less an organization in the bureaucratic sense than a movement in the most deeply religious sense.

> *A Church's call is broader than that of a denomination—its goal is not institutional maintenance but the welcoming of all into the way of Christ.*

As a Church, it is called to a holistic welcome into redeemed life. We take part in a story of salvation that is not to be understood as ours alone but as the world's story. Thus we need the widest mosaic of God's people telling the story in manifold ways. Catholicism is less a structure than it is a way of being—a way of being tied to the acceptance of God's search for each and every one of us, not simply the individual's search for God.

This reality calls us to serve one another in ways deeper than religious injunction or command. It involves the intertwining—the communion—of the fullness of our soul with the souls of all those Christ holds dear. This mystic union is lived out in the command to love one another as Christ loves us. A denomination is something we sign up for or join—Catholicism is something to which we are joined. It is a subtle but profound difference and has everything to do with the way we welcome young adults to the Church.

We are welcoming their whole being and life into communion with God's fierce love for the whole of Creation. This binds us all together in a tribe that continues this earthly pilgrimage toward the heavenly Jerusalem. It is a movement in the fullest sense of that word. The great gift of Anglicanism is that it draws together this prayerful, sacramental understanding of the whole of Creation and the Church with a Reformed respect for individual conscience and expectation of personal spiritual maturity and vitality. In other words, it is ideally positioned to engage young people who long to be part of something real and enduring and yet hold dear their own sense of individual identity and decision-making.

Young people long to be part of something real and enduring and yet hold dear their own sense of individual identity and decision-making.

In our practice here, catholicity is at the heart of our common prayer life and creedal theology. We practice a faith that is steeped in the tradition of the Church that has been formed over generations of practice and belief. We believe that the Holy Spirit not only moves in our own day but also has spoken throughout our history. Thus our contemporary practices have been shaped by the active engagement of the whole worshiping body with the Spirit over time and across human boundaries.

Catholicity is something that shapes the identity and the being of who we are as believers and servants. Without the deeper connection to the long history of our faith, we lose sight of who we are and where we are going. This is not to say that there doesn't need to be innovation in the life of the Church! On the contrary, a Catholic Anglican approach to the faith demands that we are ready to hear the voice of an active God in our midst who may be calling us in new ways. The sacramental engagement that lies at the heart of a Catholic faith demands of us an awareness of and response to the living call of God. It is in the depth of that engagement that we are drawn into the continuing work of servant leadership—as we offer all that we have and receive more of that which we are called to be as the Body.

This approach is prayerful, sacramental, authentic, and transformative. It is responsive to the great needs of the world while remaining fixed on the greater promise of God's mercy. It knows the sorrows of many, many hearts while offering the solace of the One who is love. It is mindful of our failings and sins while pledging forgiveness that is unbounded and unmerited. It is ordered and shaped by the patterns of millennia while being open to the continuing revelation breaking out in our communities of faith. In all of this it calls us out of ourselves into something more and helps us find wholeness of being.

It calls us to go deeper, to dwell longer, to trust more fully, and to forgive and be forgiven. It is concerned with our deepest sense of the Body around us, feeding us, and drawing us in through mindful engagement and self-offering. It taps into our deepest spiritual resources as a community to tackle the equally deep questions that we encounter as individuals and community.

How does such a thing take hold of us and help us know ourselves as more fully God's own?

There is a bakery I am quite fond of in New Haven called Lucibello's. On Christmas Eve, my wife and I visited Lucibello's Bakery, looking to pick up cannoli for Christmas. When we arrived, we found quite the scene! We were number fifty-two and they were on number five! No one there seemed particularly perturbed to be waiting; in fact everybody was in pretty good spirits. As I was waiting, I began to listen to the folks talking in line. One said, "Oh, I remember when this was on Chapel Street, going in as a kid." Another said, "This was always part of our Christmas." People walked out with boxes stacked high, full of pastries of all sorts.

While in line, I happened to read a piece from the *New Haven Register* on my Smartphone about the bakery. There were a number of sentences that jumped out at me about this eighty-year-old bakery. "Customers who have been frequenting Lucibello's Italian Pastry Shop for years—many long-time shoppers who came as children now visit with their own kids in tow—find a menu there today that remains true to the store's origins."

The owner says of the shop, "We just never changed anything. Everything is still made by hand, from scratch." That, he said, has been a key to the business's longevity. My favorite line in the interview was when the owner attributed the success the bakery has seen to "keeping up with tradition."

Catholicity has, at its heart, the notion of keeping up with tradition. We get to know the tradition, shape, and direction of the whole Body we are part of so that it can guide and form our lives—and so that when it needs to be guided and directed in new ways, we know what it is that we are proposing to change and what that impact might be.

There is something marvelous about the notion of studying, praying with, reading, and taking in the traditions we have as if they are living, vital things and not merely the remnants of a charming but bygone era. In an institution like the Church, keeping up with tradition is our role and duty as we curate the mysteries we have been handed. Of course, there are alterations and advances in the life of the Church that we should welcome. But there are also such departures from the history, theology, and tradition of the Church that the believer is left lost and without any significant tie to or understanding of what and who we are.

I am convinced that there is a deepening desire among many for places, experiences, and encounters that resonate with authentic history and communicate something deeper than what can be found in the mass market. Lucibello's, the bakery, is a wonderful example. It is locally owned, the owners live in the community, they are steeped in a long history, they understand the tradition, and more importantly they understand just what that tradition means to their customers.

The owner might rather like to innovate with some new pastry, and says he has slowly added an item or two here and there, but the root of their success is their understanding that their customers are coming to be part of an experience—something that hearkens back in time and place and tells a much longer story. "It is rewarding," he said, "to see the loyalty of Lucibello's customer base. The bakery has become part of family traditions for generations of local shoppers."

Keeping up with tradition does not mean mindlessly carrying out what we did the day before. It means knowing and interacting with the deeper patterns of the Christian life in such a way that the heart of the action—the thing itself—can be seen more clearly. Catholicity places a high value on this kind of relationship with a living tradition. The young adults joining us here are eager to know more of the tradition—to understand who we are, why we do what we do, where these patterns come from, and how they continue to shape our lives.

Fullness and Union

I was at a recent small group Mass with several Roman Catholics—I was invited as a guest and the celebrant was a Roman priest of some advanced age. He celebrated Mass earnestly and with a sense that something wonderful was happening in very mean circumstances. It was when we got to a period of reflections on the readings that things got interesting.

One of the readings was a rather unfortunate lesson on the role and value of women. A Roman Catholic woman said, "This reading makes me feel . . . energized." I wasn't sure what she meant by "energized" and then she said that as a woman, she was not sure what her place was in the Roman Catholic Church. She expressed a disappointment that her role seemed diminished by the structures of Roman Catholicism.

A man, well dressed and well spoken, said, "Women have always had a place in the Church." He said, "They have been nuns and have served in parish leadership roles." I was expecting him to defend the Roman Church and its stance on women's ordination. However, he then surprised me by saying, "We have had women in leadership; we have a shortage of priests; I don't understand why we aren't ordaining them!" This was met with nods and affirming statements. The sense of the entire room was that the Church was making a mistake by not ordaining women.

Then a fellow turned to me and asked, "What is it like working with women priests?" I, as a guest, did not want to get on too much of a soapbox. So I offered that it was, frankly, not much different! I said that from my point of view, a woman had borne the source of all of our sacraments and I believed that they were able to continue to bear Christ for us through the sacramental life.

Then the conversation turned to ordaining married priests. Again there was a round of affirmative nods and exclamations. Again, I was asked for my perspective as a married priest. I simply offered that I did not know what it was like not to be a married priest but that I thought it brought a fullness and awareness to my ministry that was crucial to my own life as a priest.

In other words, these folks were entirely engaged in thinking about a Catholic Church that looked different from the one they grew up with. They were looking for a Church that is Catholic in vital and living ways but offers an engagement with the modern world that their own Church seemed to struggle with. They were looking for a Church that was deeply traditional without being unresponsively traditionalist.

It is foolish to assume that all tradition is worth holding onto simply for the sake of doing so. There are things in it that are holy and true—though not all of it may be. It is the work of discernment, of a liberality of Spirit, to welcome the voices of the past into the conversation with the present. That willingness to engage both the world around us and the past while contemplating the hopes and fears of the future marks a Church that is free from authoritarian systems even as it speaks with the authority of the faith.

The Episcopal Church is ideally poised to engage the present cultural realities. We have retained the essentials—and allowed our whole Church a greater say in what we declare about nonessentials. We blend a healthy respect for the tradition with a deep regard for the present and the future. Perhaps it was the great battles within our Church between Protestant and Catholic wings that have given us an ability to focus on the core—the presence of Christ. We have practice at negotiating difference and finding not compromise for the sake of ease, but compromise that reflects the vital breadth of the Church.

I believe that many, whether Roman Catholic or from other traditions, are looking for a Church that is sacramental, connected to the early Church by tradition, has a centered life of prayer, and a dedicated engagement beyond its walls. They are also looking for a Church that honestly wrestles with the challenges of the day even as it finds the answers to those questions in that time-honored exploration of scripture, tradition, and reason.

This is a fundamentally Catholic exercise as it asks us to engage scripture with an open heart, be formed by the ongoing tradition of the Church, and through reason seek those places where the Church is in error. Young adults are not looking for pat answers or recited dogma—they are hyperinformed in some ways. Look at how a Google search

Young adults are not looking for pat answers or recited dogma

works—they are flooded with information, but it is the shape of the questions that determines the quality of the answer. Young adults are looking for a place that gives not simple answers but ways to ask the questions with greater clarity and faithfulness. Their quest is often not for answers but for belonging in a community of seeking pilgrims.

This lies at the core of a community of welcome. Any notion of hospitality must begin with the deeper question—who are we, and what are we welcoming people to? A Catholic worshiping community is one that has had its identity shaped and formed by generations of practice and prayer that shapes how we live as more deeply authentic believers. A Catholic Church is one that offers numerous ways for Christ to break into our lives and open up the story anew. Whether it is in the sacraments, in daily prayer, in the deeply rooted liturgical life, in those we serve, or in the regular patterns of our lives shaped by the liturgical year, a Catholic body is one that allows Christ to shape and form it in its fullness. Through this expansive welcome by and of Christ in our lives, we are more fully enabled to be a community that knows itself and in self-confidence can welcome others.

We are a people who walked with Christ. We are a people who met him on the shore. We are a people who betrayed him in the Garden. We are a people who saw the empty tomb. We are a people who shared on the road with him. We are a people who know him crucified, died, resurrected, ascended, reigning, and coming again. We are a people who know him in the scripture and in the breaking of bread. This sharing in the story of faith and being drawn into the Body through prayer and sacrament gives us a deeper knowledge of those who have come before us, those next to us, and those who will come after us.

Catholicity emphasizes the Body in its fullness; calling us to be more deeply aware of our fellow Christians through acts of service; calling us to a deeper union with him at the altar. Or in its drawing us into his own being at the font. Or in walking with him in the stations, hearing more of him in the Daily Office, having our lives shaped by his in the Christian year, seeing patterns of holiness in the lives of the saints. In all of this, we are being called more fully into the Body and out of ourselves. In being called out of ourselves, we are actually being drawn more fully into who we are truly called to be.

Catholicity is about not simply welcome or hearing—but about being and responding. The Church becomes a call rather than a place. All must be welcomed to our churches, but all should know they will leave transformed—Catholicity welcomes us to have our being changed and the whole pattern of our lives shaped by the ongoing life of Christ. It offers a way of knowing a living God, a living Church, a living history, and a living faith that gives young adults a way of opening the whole of their life to God's redeeming work.

This is the encounter with Christ that young people are asking for—one that changes them and forms their whole being and identity and calls them to more. The Church cannot be an exercise in esteem building alone. The state of our individual and common lives is too real for that. The challenge now is to share a Jesus we know and who knows us well enough to change us and draw us—all that we are—into newness of life. Catholicity is about wholeness—a whole community, a whole creation, and a whole self welcomed into the source of that wholeness. It shapes our entire being and demands our fullest self—it offers an authentic understanding of the Church which has, at its heart, men and women who know and love the living Christ who bids them come deeper.

Truth—*Steve Rice*

I love watching them come in the church. Eight, nine, ten of them begin every day with the same ritual. Sitting in my seat to the right of a humble side altar, I watch them make an entrance as unique as the individual. Some come early and pause to light a candle at the shrine. Others are liturgically running to their chair as the morning office begins and still some are habitually five minutes late. I'm sure this scene could be observed anywhere. Any church that offers the Daily Offices of Morning and Evening Prayer and the Mass

There is nothing we do in the liturgy that is designed to attract young adults, but they come.

would see a variety of hungry souls enter the church each and every day; the difference is, these souls are young. Over half are under the age of forty. As the priest, I am one of them.

This is not a contemporary seeker service that has come out of congregational development seminars, focus groups, or marketing firms. This is an early recitation of Morning Prayer followed by a very traditional celebration of the Holy Eucharist. There is nothing we do in the liturgy that is designed to attract young adults, but they come. For over two years they have been coming in all seasons, liturgical and meteorological. Contrary to a cynical appraisal, they are not homogenous; they are liberal, conservative, male, female, gay and straight. I think it is this universality that speaks to the heart of what is actually happening: they are looking for truth.

For our whole lives, everything has been customizable. Over our lifetimes billions of dollars have been spent by advertisers who whisper through their products that *we* are the real architects of reality. We can build anything we wish with these products as the materials and narcissism as subcontractors. Truth has been a product, just as customizable and cheap as a skin for our iPhone (which is, by now, already out of date). All authority has been fired, impeached, or overthrown by culture so all that is left is a truth defined by all and understood by none. It's not working and we're empty.

Recognition is dawning on young adults that for something to be true, it must be true for all times, in all places, and for all people. Customizable truth is not a conversation with a diverse world; it's a monologue. In a post-9/11 world made flat by technology and social media, there is no longer the luxury of living in one's own little world where truth can be contained and controlled. The need to search for that which is true and has been in all places, for all people, and in every time has been thrust upon them. The search is for catholicity.

The young adults who enter a shadowy church before work or school are finding in the ancient words and rituals of the Church an orientation of life that is universal and life-giving. We are not only learning but are finding how to love and follow Jesus Christ who is the same yesterday, today, and forever (Hebrews 13:8). We are finding stability in the Daily Office. Even if we aren't in the mood to read psalms with obscure references to a distant time and people, we understand the grounding that comes in trusting the discipline. Soon that distant time and people becomes the here and now. We are finding identity in holy water, the sign of the cross, and the sacrament of reconciliation, all of which points to our baptism where we learn who and *whose* we are. In the face of countless attempts by others to define us, we know we are sealed by the Holy Spirit and marked as Christ's own forever. In the Holy Eucharist, we are learning the joy of worshipping the only One worthy of adoration. We've seen the fruitless offerings made to things or even to ourselves. Now the boundless fruits given when joining with Christ's offering to God the Father feed us.

Catholicism is a foundation on which to build. It's been tested and tried for two thousand years. While the materials and design may be challenging, the footing of Catholicism is sure in every place, for every person, and at any time. It is the Truth.

We have embraced catholicity because it has shown us a way forward without abandoning the past. Amidst the noise and motion of finger pointing, blaming, and criticism in every arena of human life, Catholicism offers hope and how. The hope is Jesus Christ revealed in Holy Scripture, tradition, and sacraments of the Church. The how is found in a life ordered in daily prayer, the Mass, and works of mercy. As one young adult friend said, we are tired of deconstructing the deconstruction. Everything around us seems to be breaking down, including The Episcopal Church. Catholicity roots a life in building up and edifying, not tearing down. This is what a foundation does.

On this foundation we can naturally live a life that is not at odds with the faith we proclaim. There is no debate about orthodoxy vs. orthopraxy; there is just catholicity. Our orientation in prayer directs our orientation everywhere. This is why everyday there is a parade of young adults making their way in the church for ancient prayers and rituals. No matter where they are, they know where they are going. No matter who they are with, they know who they are. No matter how much the world changes, they know he who never changes. They know the Truth and they are living free.

Liturgy—*Elizabeth Costello*

As a little girl, I can remember wanting to be a married nun. I personally saw no contradiction and was frankly surprised when others did. After all, there were really only two options for a Catholic girl with a sense of religious vocation: sisterhood or motherhood. So why not try to combine them?

I loved the Roman Catholic Church. I loved the multisensory liturgy: holy water, incense, icons, the sign of the cross, genuflections. It drew all of me into a cosmic, ancient drama. I loved the many Catholic traditions, including the more wacky cultural ones expressed by my Irish Catholic grandmother. For example, upon leaving my grandmother's house, we always braced ourselves to be asperged with holy water followed by an Irish blessing. Before sprinkling us, my grandmother always reminded us that this was not just *any* holy water—it was holy water from *Lourdes* (a holy site where an apparition of the Blessed Mother was spotted). Though the vial was over fifty years old, she argued that even if you added new holy water to the mix, the old would retain its special Lourdes mojo. And as we were being doused, she'd unfailingly say: "Go forth with the grace of God! Go forth with the grace of God!"

When my family moved from the Northeast to the Southeast in my teenage years, we slowly drifted away from the Roman Catholic Church. At some point, we just stopped going to Mass. Meanwhile, most of my peers were Free Church Evangelicals who were very concerned about the state of my soul. Had I ever been "saved"? Had I ever made a conscious decision to accept Jesus Christ as my Lord and personal savior? Had I decided to follow Jesus—no turning back, no turning back? I wasn't sure, so I got sure. I got saved. And I stayed born again for most of my high school, enjoying the expressive contemporary music but especially appreciating the opportunity to worship in a racially, ethnically, economically diverse setting. Yet with all of the gifts that these communities of faith entailed, I could not shake the feeling that something was missing—though I could not quite articulate what it was.

When I went to divinity school, I began reading about liturgy. In my readings I heard an echo of some deep part of my identity. So I decided to start going to the Roman Catholic Church that my husband attended. I can still remember the joy I felt when, to my surprise, I knew all the responses. Like riding a bike despite not being in the saddle for many years, the liturgy of my youth was ingrained into my being—my mouth, my hands, my body, my heart still knew what to do. With delight I remembered the responses: "Lord, I am not worthy to receive you, but only say the word and I shall

Like riding a bike despite not being in the saddle for many years, the liturgy of my youth was ingrained into my being—my mouth, my hands, my body, my heart still knew what to do.

be healed." And while I enjoyed attending the church of my child-hood (I even contemplated being received back into the Roman Church), I was again faced with that confused, nebulous sense of reli-gious vocation I sensed as a little girl—only this time I knew becoming a married nun was not in the cards.

I saw a female priest celebrate the most Holy Eucharist for the first time in Goodson Chapel at Duke Divinity School. Immediately, my imagination for a women's religious vocation was expanded. I had literally witnessed the answer to my prayers—a very sign of pos-sibility and promise—through the life of a dignified, competent, and confident British priest named Jo Bailey Wells. As one of the first women to be ordained to the priesthood in the Church of England, almost thirty years later she would be one of the first female priests that I had ever seen. I began to learn about the Anglican tradition. I learned about the creeds and canons, the Oxford Movement and slum priests, the collects and the global Anglican Communion. It didn't take long for me to see in The Episcopal Church a way of reclaiming the catholicity that I yearned for. I began to attend an Episcopal Church right next door to where I lived in Chapel Hill, North Carolina. The services there provoked an odd sense of déjà vu. To be sure, I wasn't quite sure how to follow the little red book with a gold cross on the cover. Still, the liturgy seemed almost eerily familiar. I knew what to do with my body—genuflect, cross myself, kneel. It was all familiar, yet also different—especially with the pres-ence of a female priest!

After the service, as I made my way to the door, in the back corner I saw a shrine with an old familiar icon from childhood—a woman I knew and loved, a woman I aspired to be like, a woman that had years ago appeared in a place called Lourdes: the Blessed Mother. There in the back corner of the church was an icon of the Madonna and Child accompanied by candles. In her arms she held Christ—bearing the good news to all who passed her. As I walked out of the church, I dipped my fingers in the holy water to bless myself and laughed as I heard the echoes of my grandmother: "Go forth with the grace of God."

Reflection Questions

- *How can the Church position itself to engage young people who long to be part of something real and enduring?*

- *What traditions need to be held onto? Which ones need to be let go?*

- *How can a church be free from an authoritarian system and still speak with the authority of faith?*

- *What is the core of a welcoming community?*

- *What attracts you to worship?*

- *Do you ever feel like something is missing from your faith or faith community? What? Why?*

CHAPTER SEVEN

Mission and Evangelism

Trust and Fear

WHEN IRISH MONKS WENT ABROAD to Europe, they generally traveled in groups in which the ideal number was thirteen— the abbot and twelve monks. They called their travelling *peregrinatio pro Christo,* wandering for Christ. These monks were not going as missionaries per se. Their purpose for travel was primarily their own spiritual perfection, rather than the evangelization of others.

The monks were seeking what was called white martyrdom. It meant the sacrificing of everything to do with home in order to be like Abraham, called to go to a place that God would show. This would be their place of resurrection.

Symbolic of the type of journey that they made was that they were to travel on a boat without oar, rudder, or sail. Only the Holy Spirit would lead them to where they were to go. These are wanderers migrating not only across borders, but across the shifting ground of inner reality. Their homeland is not a physical one, but one that is rooted in the firm foundation of God.

This wandering requires that we give up what we consider security and what we fear to live without. We must trust that God is providing. In daily life we too often try to control the future, control our partners, control our circumstances, control our homes, control our destinies. The real problem—and the real joy—is that we have no control. In so many ways, these young adults joining communities such as Christ Church are such pilgrims. They are learning to give up that which they think they depend on, sacrificing security and ease, and learning to lean into their fears and give away what they imagine is power.

One of the challenges of urban ministry is asking for the help of the Spirit to help combat the twin evils of fear and loathing. Of course, work that supports justice and peacemaking is part of this as we labor to break down barriers between people and build bonds of peace and charity.

Yet the more difficult battle is to conquer those very impulses within ourselves. There are people we will encounter in ministry that will trigger both impulses in us—often at the same time. When our new interns arrived last year, we placed many of them in a challenging part of New Haven. Almost all reacted with a sense of joyful mission and immediately began to look for ways to become part of the neighborhood and to be a prayerful presence in a place that desperately needs it. A couple found it much more challenging. Fear overwhelmed them.

When our new interns arrived last year, we placed many of them in a challenging part of New Haven.

There is a profound difference between the ministry of the visitor and the ministry of the neighbor. Our interns are now engaged in a ministry of presence living among those they serve. This is no easy feat in the midst of a culture that feeds and rewards fear—a culture that sometimes subtly and often grossly teaches us to loathe difference. We are learning together what it means to be not just a visitor bringing moments of aid or comfort. We are learning what it means to take on the burdens of those we live alongside.

The ever-present strength and support of God can be found in verses throughout the Bible:

■ *Isaiah 41:10—"do not fear, for I am with you, do not be afraid, for I am your God; I will strengthen you, I will help you, I will uphold you with my victorious right hand."*

■ *Deuteronomy 31:6—"Be strong and bold; have no fear or dread of them, because it is Lord your God goes with you; he will not fail you or forsake you."*

■ *2 Timothy 1:7—"for God did not give us a spirit of cowardice, but rather a spirit of power and of love and of self-discipline."*

Urban ministry is often a ministry of facing fear. Fear of the different and what seems potentially dangerous drive our culture's response to challenging neighborhoods. We look for ways to isolate ourselves behind walls, to build a police/incarceration complex that will protect us, or to create a safety net rather than to challenge deeper systems of injustice.

The wonderful thing about fear is that it can become the fuel of love. When we conquer our fears, when God gives us the strength to go forward when we cannot do it alone, we know that we are not alone. We come to realize that grace abounds. Fear is a luxury that we cannot afford. There is too much need around us for us to spend extensive time nurturing it. Fear is a sign of a deeper ego-driven desire for self-preservation versus self-offering on behalf of the people of God. Fear is one of the many things we need to be able to offer up to God so that he can transform it and us.

Fear cannot drive the Christian response to the other. We cannot be content to say "there but by the grace of God go I"; we have to ask God to give us that spirit of power that 2 Timothy promises so that we can go—because we must go—with God's grace. Every time we act with love, it involves risk, vulnerability. Sometimes we risk our lives. More often we risk what we think is our dignity, our authority, our pride, our sense of how things should be. Being drawn into relationship is always something that is a bit frightening, often disorienting, fraught with a heady mix of terror and joy.

Real relationships cannot be entered lightly or carelessly. Real relationships, the kind that last and are deep and can withstand shocks and traumas, require attention, patience, and reverence. The best relationships always keep us a little uncomfortable, call us to be better, dare us to hope. The presence of God amongst us can be felt not only as presence, but absence. An absence of mental fictions, illusions, and false projections—a wholly discomforting, yet profoundly joyful dying of self in the presence of God—until we are not creatures of just breath and bone but of the Flesh and the Blood.

Being called into deep relationship with God or with others demands not ever-increasing comfort, but an ever-increasing willingness to be made uncomfortable. The presence of God is never a comfort or solace alone. It is a challenge—a judgment that calls us to live in the shadow of the cross. To be ever given, ever transformed, ever growing in the mind of Christ. This is essential to Christian ministry—the willingness to allow ourselves to be transformed for lives of mission.

Walking the Neighborhood

One simple way we engage the city in mission is simply to walk the Hill neighborhood in New Haven. We go door-to-door. We do not ask for anything, promise anything, or offer anything particularly grand. We ask our neighbors what they need prayers for. What deep need do they have that they would ask us to offer to God with them in our daily devotions?

The Church cannot do everything. We often overpromise and even more, in our sin and failure, underdeliver. Yet we can pray. We can pray for healing, for justice, for strength, for hope, for bravery, for forgiveness, and for love. As we walk the neighborhood and hear the needs and joys of our neighbors, I pray that it consists of many steps taken trusting in the love and grace of God.

On our walks, we met Luiz and Mike, two young men that are off drugs now and looking to share word of how Christ helped them find sobriety. They offered to help with translation so that we can better communicate with many of our neighbors. We also talked with Luke, Will, and Hector. They are guys who spend most of their day out in the park near the church. They asked for prayers and offered ideas as to how the church could be of help in the neighborhood. We also met Franklin who said his hope was for a neighborhood church that was diverse and prayerful. I also met Rosa who told me that she watches Mass on the television in the morning and evening but has no church nearby to go to. A local deli owner offered donations of food so that we can begin some community dinners.

We are beginning these walking and listening exercises in the hope that we can hear the hopes and needs of the neighborhood. In the recent past two large Roman Catholic Churches, Sacred Heart and Saint Peter's, have both closed. One parish had around 350 families and the other 225. One woman said of the closing of Sacred Heart, "There is no dialogue. They just went through the motions. Basically, it is a death sentence for us. This will have dire consequences for the neighborhood." Another said, "The poor minority neighborhoods have always been left out. . . . When you see something that's truly beautiful and has been well loved by the community threatened, it's really soul-destroying."

There is an obvious and deep need for a church in the neighborhood that hears and responds to the spiritual needs of its residents. In order to fill that spiritual hole, as well as other pastoral needs of the neighborhood, Christ Church and the ministry interns of Saint Hilda's House began to bring the liturgical tradition back to the Hill, to Church of the Ascension, a previously closed Episcopal church. Those who are part of Ascension House live, pray, learn, struggle, walk, and work alongside those whom God calls us to love—our neighbors. We are engaged in work that is in some ways new and radical and in other ways is the very essence of tradition.

Part of overcoming fear and taking root in our communities is to rediscover the heart of our authority and strength in our union with and in Christ. This begins with baptism and continues all through our sacramental life together.

The Power of the Sacramental Life

The culture we now minister in is one that forms people in ways they can scarce begin to understand. One of the most destructive messages we receive is that we are the locus of our own self-determination. Our young adults in particular are fed a constant stream of messages that both tell them they are essentially powerless but also are left on their own—to pull themselves up by their bootstraps despite the fact that they don't own their own boots. The most liberating and

The most liberating and empowering message we can offer young people is that they are not their own.

empowering message we can offer young people is that they are not their own. The course of their lives is not theirs alone and they need not rely only on their own strength. They have been brought together into a Body which can lend strength in times of weakness and which provides the decisive model for true vulnerability.

Our baptism is the ultimate and decisive empowerment. We are participants, with Christ and the Church, in a dependent coarising. Karl Barth stated, "Man is no longer single, but a couple." All of the ministers of the Church are bound in a relationship by which we are empowered as a Body and given shared authority in the name of Christ. Christian leadership is about inviting others to be part of that relationship with Christ in the sacraments.

A true priesthood of all believers is one that is founded on a shared life in Christ rather than the managerial exploitation of lines of power and authority. Sacramental living calls all of us into power-lessness before the presence of God as we invite others into that presence. Think of life and the sacraments: the vulnerability of baptism, the honesty of confession, the openness of marriage, the nakedness of last rites.

Christian ministry involves making our time with others a chance to meet the resurrected Lord as the common and ordinary are made strange, and very ordinary men and women are called into holy living. Christian ministry is not about empowerment but about presence. Dwelling in that presence in prayer, service, and worship is where our empowerment is found and where we can learn to share that power with others. We will find in the Eucharistic sharing, in the hearing of the Word, and in a life of self-giving service a deeper connection to the Christ whose story and life are ours—and ours to share. If we truly want to "empower" our congregations, we should spend more time focusing on the sacraments and less on power. Less time on our processes and more time on the Real Presence. Honest conversations about sacramental life lead to a Church that honestly understands the power it has been given.

How is God acting in the life of the heart and the community? What does it mean to live in frustration or terror? How is God acting through us and on our behalf? How is God present in our joy and our strength? Where are we failing to hear the voice of God? How do we offer our authentic selves to God when the market tries to sell us an identity? What does "We who are many are one Body" mean to us? Through honest self-examination, we are brought to convergence and out of the nadir of opposition and competition.

Life as the Church requires a willingness not to seek more power but to offer up what we think makes us strong. Some things are lost in the offering but much more is gained. God's economy is one that multiplies and magnifies even as it strips us to our core. The grace of God remakes and ever-remakes Creation and all creatures as they discern and plumb their relationship with and in God and seek to be part of the Christ offered for us. This process is the gradual emptying of attributes that inhibit God's action in us and the opening up to the filling grace of God. This offering becomes an act of self-abnegation but also of self-fulfillment as we offer to become part of the trans-forming love of Christ.

Ministry begins with Christ's sacrifice so convicting us that we can only do likewise and offer all that we are—offer all that is common and ordinary and creaturely in sacrifice. We lay it out bare for the love of God to transform as we open ourselves to his power. It is not simply Christ's power and glory which defines him (and us as Christians) but his willingness to offer up all for all. When we as leaders in the Church talk of power, Christ's is the only power that truly matters. That power was, ultimately, found in a potent pow-erlessness upon the Cross. His moment of greatest indignity was the point at which his salvific power swelled to embrace the whole of Creation—the moment at which we were truly, fully, and finally empowered. In that most vital empowerment we will find a strength that shakes loose from fear and equips us to be faithful servants.

Being and Doing—*Nathan Beall*

Our society no longer teaches us how to be present with one another. We are told to be productive: to always strive toward fixing a problem, producing a good, or providing a service. We must always be *doing*. This has driven our professional culture to a frantic, transient pace of life with little connection to our location or our neighbors. In short, we are suffocating.

I live and work at a newly forming intentional community

and restarting Episcopal parish in New Haven, Connecticut, called Ascension in the Hill. The Hill neighborhood is one of the poorest neighborhoods in New Haven, and is mostly populated by Hispanic immigrants and African-Americans. We at Ascension are not exactly sure what we are *doing* yet. As a part of the Church at large, our primary purpose is the adoration of God and the proclamation of the risen Christ. As a mission of Christ Church Episcopal in New Haven, we approach this mission from an Anglo-Catholic heritage. But we and our new neighbors in the Hill are still figuring out together how exactly this will look in our neighborhood. It involves the ebb and flow of energy and enthusiasm, trial and error, tensions, joys, frustrations, and laughter. But the first step is to be present. God becomes intimately present to each one of us in the person of Jesus Christ, and the early church bore witness to this by being present to one another in the breaking of the bread and in prayers, and by testifying to the power of God in Christ (Acts 1—4).

The following two pieces were written as reflections on this process of presence in the Hill. For me as the seminarian intern, the first marked a phase of initial excitement, and the second a phase of frustration and doubt. This eventually gave way to hope, and the cycle continues. As our ministry continues to change shape and to shape us, our commitment is to stay present: to live and pray in this neighborhood as the Church is most fundamentally called to do.

These reflections on our ministry at Ascension and my conversations with people in their twenties and thirties, both in and outside the Church, are indicative of a large movement among my generation. Many of us aren't buying that crap about being productive anymore. We are recognizing that some of the most well-paying jobs in our society are some of the most lifeless, while those who want to truly serve our communities, such as those who grow our food, teach our children, and empower the poor, are underappreciated and underpaid. So there is a new interest in just showing up. Rather than making our vocational choices by considering profit or success, we consider how we can be truly present in a community and serve its common good. Many of us, including myself, probably do not stay long enough, because we

> *Rather than making our vocational choices by considering profit or success, we consider how we can be truly present in a community and serve its common good.*

still bear the marks of a culture of transience. But we are figuring out what it means to stay with a place and a people, both in joy and frustration. I believe this growing interest in presence and consistency is what draws many young people today both to intentional communities and to the Anglican tradition. Part of the richness of Anglican spirituality is its consistency: we pray with a book, we pray every day at certain times, we say the same prayers and the same canticles and sing some of the same music that we have been for centuries. For a generation that is fed up with productivity and novelty, the stability and consistency of both intentional communities and the Anglican tradition are increasingly attractive. I hope that the following reflections reveal some of the joys and challenges behind this ministry of presence that engages so many young people today.

Affirming Life in the Hill

On a chilly Thursday evening in October of 2012, a dozen residents of New Haven gathered at the Church of the Ascension in the Hill neighborhood to discuss life in the Hill and the future of their ministry. They set their table together in the rear of the church's nave, adjacent to a wall of lit candles, watched by the eyes of Christ and Mary in the icons around them. Seated around the table were Father Robert Hendrickson from Christ Church, the three residents of the Ascension rectory, five residents of the Amistad Catholic Worker house one street over, a representative of a Latino/Latina activist organization, two residents of the Hill who were members of Living Word ministries, and myself, the seminarian at Ascension.

The evening began with a brief Gospel reading: "Look around you, and see how the fields are ripe for harvesting. . . . one sows, and another reaps." Those gathered this evening were entering into another's labor. The church had been built years ago and since dissolved as an Episcopal parish, and only recently become a mission of Christ Church. As the group prayed before the meal, Mark's sobering prayer request regarding recent violence in their neighborhood reminded those gathered of the challenges they would face in their ministry there.

But as we sat down to eat, Fr. Robert opened our conversation with a question to undermine the often negative reputation of the

Hill. "What is something in this neighborhood that has brought you joy?" The responses varied, but pointed to a common theme: there is life in this place. For many, this was exemplified by the Amistad House, which opens its doors and shares its resources with all who live in the neighborhood. But some also spoke of the way in which people in the Hill walk around at night on the sidewalks and actually speak to one another, a phenomenon less frequently encountered in more affluent neighborhoods. Someone even mentioned the life in the soil of their garden, which could grow anything. The group went on to discuss possibilities for the church to affirm this life, which included facilitating local cultural celebrations such as *La Dia de los Muertos* and a Christmas tree lighting, as well as working for justice through developing community gardens and advocating for the rights of immigrants. The energy around such ideas was tangible both during and after the meal.

What I discovered from this experience was the presence of deep and abundant life in the midst of a neighborhood that is often associated with violence and poverty. The Church's call in such a place is not to bring in "solutions" from outside to "fix" problems, but to bear witness to the life that is already present within the community, and to proclaim alongside its neighbors that, in Christ, life is stronger than death. It is at such times that those who face poverty and violence often become our teachers. "Blessed are you who are poor," Jesus says, "for yours is the kingdom of God."

Showing Up

Like every ministry, Ascension has its frustrations. I was recently sharing with Joe, a Christ Church intern, that at the end of a semester of ministry in the Hill, it still feels at times as if we are just a bunch of outsiders *talking* about doing something in a neighborhood. He nodded his head in understanding and said, "Yeah, but you showed up." I stopped to think for a moment, and then smiled. "I guess we did," I replied.

Sometimes, that's all we can really say about a ministry at the end of the day. If we have tried to help someone, or share what we have in some way, we may not always see what impact it has. A few days after that conversation, I "showed up" in the Hill with a plan for the morning: I was to pray the morning office with a friend in the Ascension nave, and then head down the street to the Catholic Worker house to help with breakfast and lead a Bible study. It turned out that the bus came late and didn't take me where I needed to go, so I got to Ascension too late for Morning Prayer and headed down to the Catholic Worker house. Over breakfast, Mark mentioned that they needed to help one of their neighbors move, so I figured I would help with that for about twenty minutes and then come back to the house for the Bible study. It turned out that their neighbor had twice as much in her apartment as we thought, including a couch that must have materialized inside the apartment, because four of us could not get it out of the doorway. We got back to the house dusty and exhausted just before Mark had to leave, so the Bible study never happened. When one of the regular Spanish-speaking attendees of the study saw me and asked what had happened, I shook my head and gave the only explanation I could in my broken Spanish, "Fue un mañana loco." ("It was a crazy morning.")

Nothing went as I had planned that day, and I certainly did not get the results I was expecting. But I did show up. That's what the folks at the Catholic Worker house in the Hill did eighteen years ago: they just showed up and stayed, and they have changed people's lives. I think if we reflect on the Incarnation, we see that it's about God showing up for us in a completely unassuming way. Maybe that is the revolution to which God in Christ is calling each of us; to just show up and be present, especially in times and places in which the rest of the world doesn't.

Deeper than Chaos—*Adam Trettel*

The Episcopal Diocese of Southern Ohio printed one of the earliest posters for refugee resettlement in the United States in 1938. It is a drawing of Mary and Jesus riding on a donkey, with Joseph walking alongside, against a dark blue moonlit sky. The text reads: "In the name of these refugees, aid all refugees." It is a fascinating and fitting parallel to draw; Jesus and his parents were refugees in Egypt after Herod ordered the slaughter of infants in Roman Palestine.

In the aftermath of the Second World War, individuals in the

American church helped to turn provisional acts of charity—opening homes to refugees, cooking meals, organizing clothing drives—into an organized process. That war had made millions of people stateless; yet still today, there are fifteen million refugees in the world, and the number is currently growing due to the war in Syria. Each year 75,000 are given an opportunity to begin life anew in the United States, through a complex procedure overseen by the State Department, the United Nations, and a myriad of charitable organizations. As a member of the Episcopal Service Corps in 2011–12, I served for ten months as a housing and donations coordinator at one of these organizations, IRIS (Integrated Refugee & Immigrant Services), in New Haven, Connecticut.

Most of our clients at IRIS were from Iraq, Eritrea, and the Congo. Often they had been living in other host countries or in refugee camps for years. Some had previously owned multiple homes and had servants; others had never seen a shower or a gas stove; almost all had taken out a loan to buy a one-way plane ticket to America. In their first few weeks they would apply for food stamps, cash assistance, jobs; the adults would enroll in English classes, the children in local schools. Everyone went to the doctor. After one year they would be eligible for Green Cards and, after five, U.S. citizenship.

My job was to set up their apartments according to a U.N. checklist. I had a pickup truck, a volunteer cohort of teenage boys and two female college athletes, and a very limited budget. We relied mainly on local thrift stores and charitable donations to supply the apartments: Girl Scouts packed sandwich bags with toothpaste, nail clippers, washcloths; a Jewish primary school donated toys and clothing; universities donated old dorm-room furniture. These resources were constantly depleted and continually refilled. During my time at IRIS the housing team set up apartments for around two hundred people.

Our policy was not to ask clients about their background, but many wanted to talk.

An Iraqi man held graduate degrees from universities in France and the U.K. and had worked as a prominent scientist; he fled Baghdad with his wife after terrorists murdered his teenage son and abducted one of his daughters. An Iranian family converted to Christianity in Teheran; the wife quit the country with her teenage son and daughter after her husband disappeared. A Congolese man had lived in UN camps for nearly fifteen years with his wife and seven children, spending his days searching for firewood to cook dinner for his family.

We all read stories like this in the newspapers. But it is different to hear it firsthand, to know how much responsibility you have over these people's lives.

There were good stories too. Our office cleaner, a refugee, was reunited with his two young daughters after being separated for several years. A Congolese woman tracked down her husband through the United Nations, who had told her before that he had been killed; she spoke to him on the phone and was working with our legal department to bring him to the U.S.

And clients brought food to share at the office every day. We always told them to save their money, and they kept bringing more, pretending not to understand. "I was held in a chair and told to have tea," a case manager said about a home visit.

It is difficult for me to summarize my time working with refugees at IRIS. If I could compress it into a phrase it would be this: I am astonished by the resilience of our clients, our volunteers, and our staff.

Looking back, I also wonder how such an effort happens at all. Refugee resettlement is chaotic, logistically and emotionally difficult for everyone involved. It suffers from a constant lack of funding, requires armies of translators, and is rife with confusion and false starts for both clients and staff. But it keeps happening. *It keeps happening.* Even when staff were tired and wanted to go home, even when we worried over particular clients' mental health or job prospects, or when logistics broke to pieces—it all kept happening. Things worked out. Why?

I don't think there is an easy answer to that question. But I believe there is something mysterious and very hard about human love at the center of it all. One of the prayers for mission in the service of Morning Prayer puts it this way: "O God, you have made of one blood all peoples of the earth, and sent your blessed Son to preach peace to those who are far off and to those who are near."[15] Something deeper than war, or violence, or famine links human beings together, something deeper than chaos and deeper than confusion. The peace that

---

[15] Book of Common Prayer, 100.

Jesus brought to the world has no boundaries; it breaks down borders; it can see no limits. My time at IRIS helped me to understand that in a more concrete way.

Encountering God—*Eric Gregory*

Where is it that young adults fit into current Western models of mission and evangelism that the Church currently offers?

The easy, if slightly flippant, answer to this question is: nowhere. Young adults are, far more often than not, excluded from vestries, boards, and councils that end up making decisions about the practices of the Church. To be fair, according to many of the statistics most often quoted in Protestant-based studies, young adults have a tendency to leave the Church after confirmation, to return only after having children of their own—which makes including us in decision-making structures more complicated and difficult than it might otherwise be. Yet even this, perhaps, should be a clarion call for the Church; our young people are distancing themselves from the most important community-building enterprise the world has ever known. Without attempting to articulate all of the reasons that this might be the case (we have the Pew Research Center and other statistical analysis groups doing this already), I wanted to offer a few ways in which the Church might enter into a deeper relationship with young adults both inside and outside of her congregations.

> *Young adults are, far more often than not, excluded from vestries, boards, and councils that end up making decisions about the practices of the Church.*

It is important to understand the theological nature of mission and evangelism to set the groundwork for what it is the Church should be asking of its young people, or what it is the Church should be doing in order to incorporate young people into its midst. Mission and evangelism are central to what it means to be the Church. Looking at the terms historically and biblically, mission can easily be defined as what the Church is called to do and who it is called to be; and evangelism is how the Church goes about this doing and being.

In terms of mission, the Episcopal Church has heard quite a bit (most recently before, during, and after the 77th General Convention in July 2012) about new or emerging ways of doing church that do not subscribe to the parish model that has been in place for the last few centuries. We're encouraging our priests and lay people to explore new ways of being the Body of Christ, and steering our seminarians away from the idea that full-time curacies, associate positions, or even becoming a rector are in their future. We are trying to figure out what a twenty-first-century expression of authentic Christian experience looks like. Some of this conversation, despite not including many young adults, has actually been in the name of reaching young adults with a message of the love of Christ—young adults who don't seem to be a part of the Church at this point in time.

These conversations and creative expressions of Christian faith and community do indeed seem necessary and helpful as a shrinking liberal Protestantism seeks to remain true to its faith and calling. Yet, on the ground, despite our concerns about the future, parishes are where ministry happens and parishes are where our young people are not. How can we address this? How can we make our parishes more engaging to young adults? How can we invite the young adults who are already connected to these parishes to become the pillars of faith that we would all like them to be?

In a recent lecture delivered at Berkeley Divinity School at Yale, the Rev. Carol Anderson, a parish priest with over forty years experience, articulated five things that thriving, vital parishes and congregations include: thoughtful, transcendent worship; articulated vision for developing people into disciples of Jesus; identifying and equipping lay people for ministry; effective outreach; and expectancy in prayer. These, I believe, also speak to the needs young people have for critical engagement and full inclusion in the life of the Church catholic.

While many parishes have honed in on discipleship, lay ministry, outreach, and prayer—which again are incredibly important and necessary—my own experience has been with a parish that makes worship central to its articulation of the mission of the Church, seeing it as an instrument of evangelism in addition to its central purpose of adoration and praise. Worship, when done well, and not for a human audience but a divine one, changes people's lives.

This is never more evident for me than when talking with young adults after Christ Church, New Haven's Sunday evening Compline service. The church is dark, save for candles at the high altar and at a small shrine outside of the rood screen. Incense makes even this minimal illumination murky and clouded, making it nigh impossible to see anyone on either side of you in the pews. The choir sings and chants Renaissance settings of the service from the loft, invisible to the congregation. There is no sermon, no greeting, no announcements, no offering (aside from plates set out at the entrances), no coffee hour, no participation aside from the silence in one's heart while cantor and choir sing. There is only darkness, light, silence, and song. And despite this—despite refraining from doing the things that many parishes try to incorporate in order to make themselves more relevant or allow them to connect with newcomers—Compline is one of the most well-attended services in all of the city on Sundays. The kicker? The majority of those in attendance are young adults under the age of thirty. Perhaps as we simultaneously seek to understand what the Church will and should look like in the future, we also invest heavily in the two things Church does that no other community-building organization can do: worship the Triune God with all reverence and sincerity (mission), and invite others to encounter the living God (evangelism).

The point of mission and evangelism is the ability of the Church to show people Jesus Christ, and we do this by living, doing, showing, believing, and confessing. Worship, when thoughtfully planned and lovingly executed, has the ability to do what even our lives and our words cannot: it brings people to Jesus in authentic encounter.

Reflection Questions

- *What do you fear to live without?*
- *What is the difference between the ministry of the visitor and the ministry of the neighbor?*
- *How do you overcome your fears, personally and as a church?*
- *How does focusing on the sacraments empower people in their ministry?*
- *How is God acting in the life and heart of your community?*
- *What threads do you find in the stories of Nathan Beall, Adam Trettel, and Eric Gregory?*

CHAPTER EIGHT

Seeking and Searching

Authentic Expressions—*Jordan Trumble*

ONE OF THE RICHEST ASPECTS of the Episcopal Church is the amazing breadth of our tradition. Although the Holy Scriptures, The Book of Common Prayer, *The Hymnal 1982*, and a variety of supplemental liturgical resources unite us, no two congregations are quite the same. We have parishes with pipe organs and choirs and parishes with praise bands and projector screens; parishes with East-facing altars, parishes with West-facing altars, and parishes that worship in the round with the altar in the middle; we have congregations that use incense like their salvation depends on it and congregations who would never even think of incorporating it into worship. Like with its liturgical practices, the Episcopal Church also comprises a variety of missional and outreach practices, from trips to foreign lands to running social service programs out of a church's own buildings. In short, we have as many interpretations of what it means to be part of the Episcopal Church as we do Episcopal parishes and, indeed, probably as many as we do members. Each church community has gifts and talents that make it uniquely suited for particular ministries. In a church that has so many different understandings of what it means to be an Episcopalian, who is right? Are the praise-music-singing, communing-in-the-round folks the ones who are down with the hip trends? Or do the East-facing, thurible-wielding Anglo-Catholics have the answer to the all of the church's problems?

As a church and as a society, we are quick to dismiss that which is old as being irrelevant and to dismiss that which is modern because it is untested. We are caught in the tension between the past and present, between whom we have been and who we feel God is calling us to be. We are convinced that because church attendance is declining, we must abandon much of what we have done in the past in favor of that which is newer and hipper. Yet I contend that this very question of who is right and who is wrong, a question we are often all too quick to answer, is not even a valid question for us to be asking. Instead of creating dichotomies of what is right and wrong, what attracts and what drives away, the question we should be asking is whether or not our practices are authentic expressions of who we are and how we understand God to be working among us.

When I hear claims that older liturgical practices are outdated or that newer practices are untested and thus useless, I am reminded of an exchange I had several times with my mother as I was growing up. I was a socially awkward child and would at times yearn to be friends with people I thought were cooler. As many adolescents do, I tried to change things about my personality to engender the liking of others. Each time this happened I would end up unhappy because I wasn't being authentically myself and my mother would remind me that I shouldn't try to change myself to please others; anyone worth having in my life would appreciate me for who I was. She would tell me not to try to sell myself as something I wasn't. Invariably, I would roll my eyes at my mother and tell her that she was only saying that because it was a parent's moral or ethical obligation to say such things to their upset child.

We are so concerned with attracting young adults that we often don't stop long enough to ask if the things we are doing to attract young adults are authentic reflections of who we are and what we believe.

Yet when I think of the church, its mission to attract my generation, and its arguments over what young adults want, my mother's words come back to me. We are so concerned with attracting young adults that we often don't stop long enough to ask if the things we are doing to attract young adults are authentic reflections of who we are and what we believe.

When we make changes, are they because we think people will like us or are they because we feel God is calling us to change? Are we conforming to the world's standard for us or to God's standard for us?

More than perhaps anything else, young adults crave authenticity. In so many aspects of our lives, we are being sold images of what is hip and trendy; the last place we want to find this superficial practice of conforming to what is cool is in church, a place where we learn not to conform to the world but where we are called to be authentically grounded in our identity as children of God and members of the Body of Christ.

When young adults look for a church, we aren't looking for a church that feels cool. We want a church who knows who it is. We look for a church whose identity isn't just rooted in what it does but whose identity is rooted in Jesus Christ. We want a church whose worship and mission is a natural and authentic progression of its faith and theology. We don't want a church that changes who it is simply to attract different people but rather a church that allows itself to be changed by the Holy Spirit and by the gifts and talents of those who come through its doors.

Sincerity—*Matthew Larson*

It can be hard not to like some things that have been a part of your life for a significant amount of time. Church parishes can definitely be one of those things. Although there is no doubt that I have a degree of bias toward my parish, there is also no doubt that if I were born in a different place or raised on a different religion, I would not have all the same beliefs, or participate in religion as I do now. Having only belonged to two different churches for the vast majority of my life, Christ Church is definitely well intertwined in me.

There are many important factors that make me continue to love the church, and the people engaged in its many facets. The largest of these would be sincerity. There is no fooling around at Christ Church. You can see the love and energy put into the church whenever you walk onto the grounds, or experience a service. From the intricate carvings at the altar, to the well-worn utensils of the soup kitchen, it is an amazing thing to see the physical products of so many people's love so tightly condensed into one place. Not to say that it takes physical things to show that there is love in a place, but there is no doubt that it contributes to this highly inspiring environment.

Another similar but distinct aspect is the High Church practices observed at Christ Church. The actions within the liturgy portray the same love that can be seen physically in different ways. High Church liturgy provides a more distinct form of ritual that is effective and extremely moving to me. I enjoy worshiping in this way, as it provides such a strong emotional pull. In modern times, in our everyday lives, it often feels like we lack this sense of intimacy we may have once had. I value being able to reconnect with that. This can compliment our current lives full of ease and efficiency. It feels like our younger generation lacks any amount of time long enough to have this sort of dynamic experience with much of anything today. We are all consumed by modern high-paced conveniences, but through making the time, we can become more in tune with the passions of generations past.

Sometimes there seems to be a disconnect between children and their understanding of the religious values that their parents might have. It often seems like the reason for this is the lack of explicitness that children are exposed to when it comes to religion. A friend of mine recently shared some of the religious children's videos she watched as a child. I was stunned by how dry many of them were. Attempts like these to show religion as a bland message of general care for each other—even for children—does not ideally represent the awesomeness of life and the love of God. For me, many parts of Sunday school did prove to be insightful, but the most influential and enlightening moments for me definitely occurred during church services. Christ Church never ceases to enlighten and illuminate the young and old.

I believe that one of the major incentives of belonging to a parish like Christ Church revolves around a sense of urgency. In a world where so many people seem to be less connected with traditional religion, will people forget why we attend in the first place? I feel that at a place such as Christ Church, there is the best of everything. A traditional service that is rich in ancient tradition, along with a denomination's belief system that supports modern social values. I feel that it is in environments like these that we may have the best chance at keeping these traditions alive and thriving, helping to retain the love that so many people have already contributed to. An environment where compromise is implemented in the most appropriate manner possible: a strong support of core values presented in a dynamic way, along with evolving to deal with the social issues we face here and now. Christ Church is, in a word, real.

Holiness—*Brigid Davis Snow*

When I arrived in New Haven three and a half years ago, it was my first time "church shopping." I did not grow up in a church, but in college I found myself at the heart of a very close-knit (and fairly liberal) Catholic community.

At the end of college, our chaplain sent all of the seniors a heartfelt e-mail warning us that the path to finding a spiritual home as a young adult would be an arduous one. Nothing will feel like college, she warned, and it will be a difficult and painful process to find a parish to call home. Not only would we deal with the same realities as any person moving to a new place—in a sea of options, looking for the perfect storm of liturgical style, location, and social politics, being a stranger—but as young adults, most parishes would not be built around or for people our age.

I braced myself for the struggle, knowing that my "perfect storm" would be particularly difficult. I still considered myself Roman Catholic, and sought a home with rather orthodox theology, a requirement of beautiful but unfussy liturgics, and opportunity for active membership while being a queer woman. To make matters worse for myself, I was fairly certain that my ecclesiology was not at all Roman, but I was not willing to give up catholicity or high sacramental theology. I learned the term "Anglo-Catholic" that summer, but had no practical experience of what that meant or looked like. Thankfully, I happened to have chosen a law school in a city with an historic parish solidly set in the Anglo-Catholic tradition and spent a month attending Roman Catholic Mass as well as Christ Church's Solemn High Mass and Compline. There I found, providentially, the match of catholicity without authoritarianism, orthodox theology without reactionary politics, and serious liturgical beauty without fussiness.

The most apparent draw, and the one most noticeable to visitors, was the commitment to the beauty of holiness and the holiness of beauty. While appreciating the importance of a variety of aesthetic offerings (as different individuals will have different experiences of what brings them closer to God), I have never been happy in a Christian community that does not give special attention to aesthetic quality of worship. Worship that takes half-measures in liturgy does insult to God, who created the universe in beauty, and to ourselves, as creative beings made in God's image and naturally drawn to that harmony of colors, sounds, and fragrances that reflect the harmonious nature of God. Similarly, liturgy that only engages the auditory and not the other senses neglects a large portion of the means we are given by which to experience Creation—sensory faculties that we share with the Incarnate Christ. To do all this without being fussy, or trying to revert to a static moment in history, should be the aim of all worship.

What I sought more deeply, though, was a church that takes theology seriously (and remains faithful to orthodoxy) without being reactionary. I am, through my interests and learning style, particularly interested in theology, but I do not mean that churches need regular disputations on justification and sanctification. I mean that the leaders of the parish should be able to think rigorously about theology and be able to explain why our worship or beliefs are as they are in meaningful terms. A parish needs commitment to religious education, both for youth and for adults, in ways that encourage continual learning and critical thinking about faith. At the same time, being orthodox does not require being reactionary; truth is beyond our understanding, and any attempt to box it into shallow categories and not allow room for growth results in heresy, not orthodoxy.

> A parish needs commitment to religious education, both for youth and for adults, in ways that encourage continual learning and critical thinking about faith.

Finally, I felt strongly then, and do so even more now, about belonging to a parish that worships on more than Sunday. At the bare minimum, the availability of the Daily Office offered during the week. Morning and Evening Prayer have come to feel like the rhythm of worship life, and even if I am not able to attend in person, the prayers that are being offered and the scripture that is being read make for a stronger parish that is more closely knit into the life of the Church. Daily Eucharist does this to a deeper extent. As a Roman Catholic, I took the presence of daily Eucharist for granted. Within the Episcopal Church, this is a rare practice. A parish that offers the Eucharist on more than just Sundays (or worse, occasional Sundays) signals to me that this parish takes the sacrament seriously as the means by which we are one with the Church throughout the world and throughout history.

All of these factors are, upon reflection, aspects of being one, holy, catholic, and apostolic. While orthodox theology or liturgical sensibilities can at times turn into the quibbles that divide us, upon closer look they are, in fact, the means by which we find common ground with the Church throughout the world and throughout time. While finding a community with young adult potlucks and service opportunities is valuable, and finding a church with quality preaching can help parishioners lead better Christian lives, I do not belong to a church as a social club or a Bible study group. I look for a parish to be the means by which I can circumvent denominational, geographical, and temporal distance, to be connected, through local corporate prayer, with the mystical Body of Christ, the blessed company of all faithful people.

To Be Taken Seriously—*Laurel McCormack*

Between the start of my high school years and up to this point, I have been deeply involved in a varied list of congregations, from a nondenominational megachurch to a twelve-person Quaker/liturgical church and several others in between. Some of my elders probably wrote me off as a young "church consumerist," bopping around to whatever services offered the particular form of worship, fellowship, and theological teaching that I desired at the time. Rather than confess to that charge, I will reflect here on how my experiences informed what I believe young adults honestly want and need in church. Some churches deterred me from developing into a faithful member of their congregation and helped me understand how my friends, sitting on the fence of spiritual interest and ambiguity, were "turned off" by their own church experiences. Other churches welcomed and drew me in, and I beheld treasures that my friends miss out on when they stop giving church a chance: encountering God through all that the members of that Christ-filled community have to teach.

I have known Christ most fully in churches that took me seriously as a young adult. I want my friends who are sitting on the fence to be exposed to these churches. I want these churches to know that they can draw my friends in. In these churches, I was offered Christian responsibility, discipline, and intergenerational community.

Churches take young people seriously when they trust them with responsibilities and leadership within the church. Our teachers, professors, and supervisors ask us to take responsibility for our growth and stretch our ability and knowledge. Confusingly, when we enter a church, the adults around us seem to expect and sometimes encourage us to take up the ways of childhood afresh, lest they scare us away by asking too much of us. During my freshman year of high school, I was involved in a youth group where our parents served us snacks each week while we simply showed up and partook of the smorgasbord of activities, sermons, and worship that the adult youth ministers had prepared. The only time we were ever "involved" in the youth services was during the first few minutes when we played icebreaker games. At this youth group, I leaned back, learned little, and eventually stopped attending. The church seemed the main place Jesus should be reaching out to me; when adults in the church ignored or expected little of me, I felt that there was nothing in me that Christ was interested in and that I had nothing worth sharing with other believers.

Asking young adults to garner meaningful responsibility within the church scares us away far less often than it flatters and interests us, especially when an older adult in the church notices particular strengths and finds a way for us to serve through them. When a friend brought me to her "Uth" group later in high school, I noticed that students who had attended for at least two months each served according to their interests and gifts during the youth meetings; the hospitality team was in charge of snacks, the music team in charge of selecting and rehearsing the hymns, and so on. When it was noticed that I spoke rarely but thoughtfully and loved to delve into practical theological topics, the youth minister asked me to preach during a youth service the following year. Make no mistake; there were many other teenagers in the group who were far more biblically literate, wise, and engaging than I was. I certainly was not a "safe choice" for a leadership role, and yet I can still recount how my paradigms about Christian hope shifted during the weeks I prayed and prepared my sermon under the guidance of the minister. This church drew young adults into its community through responsibility and leadership, in the belief that we become disciples of Christ when much is expected of us and when we are asked to step up, that we best discover our beliefs about God when we must articulate them, and that we learn how to follow Christ only when we are called upon to actively love and serve those around us.

Churches take young people seriously when they expect and help them to grow in spiritual and religious disciplines. On our "Uth" retreats, we were led through a humble, prayerful, and joyful thirty-six-hour fast. We served alongside the undocumented immigrants who lived largely hidden in a wealthy part of our county. I learned under the direction of my Bible study leader how to make full use of the cross-reference system in my Bible, and over those few years, my biblical literacy rapidly improved. Churches fear forcing solid spiritual food on young people when they are still only ready for milk. Yet many churches do young people a disservice by shying away from training in spiritual disciplines, while most young adults are unaware that they are ripe for deeper spiritual teaching. When the church babies young adults, is it any wonder that they remain spiritual infants?

I am someone who needs spiritual training to encounter God; yet far from feeling constricted or boxed in by the disciplines several congregations taught me, I felt an increasing spiritual freedom over time. I was taught the basic steps of the dance that many beautiful souls had done before me in their paths toward knowing Christ: prayer, biblical study, Communion, fasting, reflection, writing, community prayer, community, community, community. . . . And once I had learned the basics, I could recast, reimagine, reorder these steps in my own dance toward trying to know the Lord more fully. I came to see those churches that were not afraid to teach young adults these steps as wellsprings of truth on how to approach and encounter God. They expected us to develop a steady, lasting faith that could carry us into mature adulthood, and for most, this requires sharing with us the disciplines that make up the "bread and butter" of Christian life.

Churches take young people seriously when they cultivate intergenerational Christian community and companionship in which the younger are not seen or treated as lesser disciples. Young adults are both wise and foolish in that we, like the kindergartener or octogenarian, have both everything to learn about faith and God and yet have much to contribute that no one else can. For the first two years of college, I attended a small church with my group of college friends. After attending and serving in the children's ministry on Sunday mornings for a year, most of the adults who also served still did not know our names or speak to us beyond a weak smile and a "good morning." Our university Bible study was held strictly separate from the "adult" Bible studies, and we were never invited to the group family lunches at nearby restaurants after services or to the layperson meetings on the future of the congregation. This congregation wanted to "have" a token group of university students and did the minimum amount to "keep" us, but whatever we had to offer as young Christians was treated as only edifying enough for other young Christians to witness, and certainly not worth bothering the older congregants about.

> Young adults are both wise and foolish in that we, like the kindergartener or octogenarian, have both everything to learn about faith and God and yet have much to contribute that no one else can.

I was redeemed when one Sunday morning during my sophomore year, I wandered into a tiny congregation's service. I was often the youngest congregant in attendance by twenty, and more typically, fifty years. And though I was in the midst of spiritual, familial, advocate, and academic giants, they did not despise my youth and instead valued anyone who "set[s] the believers an example in speech and conduct, in love, in faith, in purity" (1 Timothy 4:12). They lived as if they were the ones blessed by my participation in their church rather than the other way around. The whole shape of my life changed as this congregation drew me in; members would show up on my doorstep ready to take me out to ice cream during finals week or to bring me to their family's Easter dinner. No longer able to travel themselves, they relished the times I Skyped them when I was studying abroad and asked me to "preach" and reflect on my experiences abroad at Sunday services after each of my returns. Nearly every week, someone would hug my neck and ask some variation of, "Aren't you getting bored of being around all us old people?" and I would counter, "Can you really be so glad to have a smart ass college kid in your wise little group?" We would then immediately move on to updating about family situations, wondering over a theological question from the sermon, or making plans together for the coming week, and these were answers enough to them and to me.

In this and in other churches I've discussed, congregants truly valued me as a fellow disciple, however youthful. I want to be a part of a church where the congregants are constantly in the growing pains of learning, recommitting to, and flourishing under spiritual discipline; where they first shrink from and then unexpectedly rise to the responsibilities within their church after realizing they do (still/after all) each have gifts to be offered to Christ and to community; and where they are willing to experience all of this alongside the young Christians in their midst in the hopes of being changed and shaped by Christ and by their relationships with one another.

A Relationship with God—*Mason Shefa*

What I looked for in a church dramatically changed between the time I was attending my parents' church and when I had entered an Episcopal church for the first time. I grew up in an evangelical Presbyterian megachurch in which average Sunday attendance approached three thousand. It was the only church I had ever attended and thus I had a limited notion of the diversity of Christian religious experience and worship. What "worked" for me at the megachurch would become the things that I sought out in other churches, not knowing of the range of other possibilities from other denominations that could enhance my worshiping experience. Most of all, however, I felt that I never had a close relationship with God, and I wanted that to change.

That change happened when I entered Christ Church, New Haven one Sunday in October of 2011. The worship style was unlike anything I had ever experienced. The ministers and servers were elegantly garbed in colorful fabrics with intricate patterns. Clouds of incense seemed to rise like a spirit, mingling with the light of the stained-glass windows, and encircling various objects such as a magnificently adorned book, and a large glowing cross. The altar party seemed to be moved not by their own incentive but by God himself, in a flow that evoked the motion of angels. Time seemed but a distant concept; the Mass seemed to happen beyond its very existence. Bells would ring and cause motion, who's motion caused yet another bell to ring. Every motion and movement was caused by one before it, and caused some after it. A line from Psalm 96 came to my mind upon reflecting on the service, "Worship the Lord in the beauty of holiness" (Psalm 96:9, Book of Common Prayer). I was engaged in the service using all of my senses: I could see the beauty of holiness; smell the whirling, fragrant incense; hear the chiming bells and angelic voices of intonations and polyphony; feel the wafer and chalice touch my hand and lips; and taste the elements of Holy Communion commingling on my tongue. All one had to do was close his eyes and instantly he could imagine himself in heaven, experiencing the splendor of God.

After this first experience at Christ Church, I had to return. The worship style awakened in me a more profound and mysterious form of devotion that reached into the depths of my soul and seized me at my core. A latent yearning for such mystical devotion had been just under the surface but had never been fulfilled nor even acknowledged until I discovered this form of worship. The years of longing for a more intimate relationship with God was put to an end in finding fulfillment in this new experience. While I felt at first that my encounter with Christ Church was fortuitous, I have come now to believe that it was actually God's answer to my seemingly ceaseless prayers for his presence in my life.

I return to Christ Church every Sunday because I appreciate its witness to many different forms of prayer, spoken and unspoken. I have learned that prayer does not necessarily entail words, but can also include silent meditations on beautiful things offered to God, or becoming enraptured by transcendent hymns. It was not long before I decided to join the Acolyte Corps. Being a part of the movement of the service is also, for me, a form of prayer. Holding the cross reminds me of Christ carrying the burden of all our sins on his back in the form of the cross upon which he was to be crucified. Holding a candle reminds me of how Christ is the "light of the world" (John 8:12) to lighten the Gentiles (Luke 2:32). Swinging a smoking censer reminds me of the dispersive presence and formlessness of the Holy Ghost, and of our prayers which gently waft to the Father above.

I am still in a transition period with regard to which theological doctrines I believe and which I reject. Coming from a strict Calvinist background, I was not given much room to think for myself on what I believed. What draws me to the Episcopal Church, most especially at this transitional time in my life, is the fact that there is much more space given to theological variance; besides the unifying fundamentals of the ancient creeds, there are no long-winded confessions concerning the will or the nature of the Lord's Supper that one is bound to believe in. This allows me to have conversations with people who, though we worship in the same space, hold a wide variety of theological positions, thereby fostering my own sense of what I believe. It is also, however, reassuring to know that though we do hold a wide variety of positions on certain things, we are all united by the words of the Book of Common Prayer. Every Sunday, I am comforted knowing that other Episcopalians around the world, however diverse we may be, are all sharing in the weekly experience of the eloquent rhythm of the words of the prayer book. Finally, though I may not live in New Haven forever, I will always remember Christ Church as the place in which I drew near to God and never looked back.

Intentional Community—*Steve King*

Within the past several years, the Church broadly and The Episcopal Church specifically have made focused efforts to provide opportunities for young adults to contribute to its life and ministry. In my experience, in the past this has included attempts to contemporize worship and endlessly program youth and young adult groups so that it can become a distraction or turn-off for some. As the Church has continued to emphasize young adult ministry, it has in some ways moved away from the latest trends and toward ancient practices that have always drawn people of all ages to it. Indeed, these comments do not seek to reflect on contemporary and traditional worship or the latest programs but instead on what has always and what will continue to sustain the life of the Church—an authentic, faithful, and transformed community with a strong focus on prayer and worship of God as well as service to those in need.

When I first began attending church (at an Episcopal church) in Lawrence, Kansas, it was a contemporary music service that sustained my worship life with God. However, as a high school student it was not the music that drew me to return repeatedly to the church. Instead, it was the sense that the people gathered were genuinely encountering Christ and living transformed lives because of it. I frequently still seek that sense of authentic worship that was true to that community's life and practice. But it was nothing the community *did* that created this sense that my soul still longs for. Instead, it was who the community was—faithful followers of God who experienced worship as a time to come closer to their Creator and then to move out into the world, transformed by this.

After graduating college, I moved to New Haven, Connecticut, where I began a year of service as an intern with Saint Hilda's House, as part of the Episcopal Service Corps. At that time, we lived in the rectory of Christ Church, New Haven, where the seven interns lived as a community focused on a rule of life, prayer, service, and worship. Not only did we all volunteer at different organizations throughout the city, we also spent our time in communal meals, prayer, and involvement with the corporate worship life of the parish. This Anglo-Catholic parish embodies in many ways the opposite of every other worship experience I had previously been a part of. Yet it possesses everything that continually drew me to the church in Lawrence.

In its efforts to reach young adults, it seems as though the Episcopal Church has out-thought itself and missed the gift it already possesses. In fact, that which young adults (and all people, really) crave within their lives is a deep sense of authentic community. The Episcopal Church already offers this and, in addition, provides space to encounter God and God's transforming love and grace. Learning this simple, yet somewhat foreign fact when I was living in New Haven was one of the greatest surprises of my life in an intentional community. That is, young adults want to go to church. This is not necessarily a profound realization that I expected to have and yet is one that I (and the Church as a whole) continually forget. It is not that church is no longer relevant to society today. However, the Church has not offered and communicated fully why it has always and will always be relevant and necessary. One of the Church's missteps in its efforts to attract young people is moving beyond itself into something that is no longer who it once was. Living in intentional community showed me that the practices that long sustained believers still continue to sustain the faithful to this day. The Church's greatest gift to young people is not becoming something different than who it is and has been but instead, the greatest gift is in sharing and inviting people to be a part of that which has given life to so many throughout the centuries.

Living in intentional community showed me that the practices that long sustained believers still continue to sustain the faithful to this day.

In my own life, experiencing these gifts from the church and the community within it has not only called me to a greater involvement within the life of the Church but also to service outside of its walls. I am currently in seminary preparing for ordained ministry in The Episcopal Church. Even as someone who has felt called to ordained ministry for most of my life, I have always been anxious and even nervous to share my faith and to invite someone to church. Knowing that God's grace and love are the greatest gift I have ever received and that they need to be shared with the world inspired me to work with the homeless and hungry and those in jail. Yet it was the experience of intentional community—a group of people focused on communal life and prayer—that taught me that people want to be a part of an authentic, believing, and transformed community. Young people are a part of this craving too. I also learned that this craving is for something substantial—not watered down or full of apologies. Having seen this prove to be true several times in my year of service, I feel more fully formed to not only share my faith with others but to do my part to move the Church into a better understanding of this need so that it can do the same. Young adults want to be invited to the life of these authentic communities and bring a renewed energy that can not only transform the church but also help in God's work of transforming the world more fully into the image of God. It is for the Church now to recall who it has always been and the gift it has always shared, not to just move beyond itself. The invitation to an authentic, faithful community is a powerful one and one that young adults yearn for. My prayer is that, empowered by the love of God, we may always make this invitation and, in doing so, remain open to being transformed ourselves.

Reflection Questions

- *How is the church caught in the tension between the past, present, and future?*

- *When changes are made in your church, are they because you think people will like them or because God is calling you to change?*

- *How can today's church be "real"?*

- *Why is the path to finding a spiritual home an arduous one for young adults (or anyone)?*

- *Name some examples of how you or your church take young people seriously.*

- *What draws you to participate in a community?*

CHAPTER NINE

Communities Changing Individuals

Discernment—*Jordan Trumble*

A T FIRST GLANCE, THE QUESTION of how communities can change individuals seems almost antithetical to the idea of living or working in community. After all, isn't community all about being selfless and thinking of everyone else? Don't communities stamp out individualism in favor of a common identity? Aren't communities concerned with "we" and not with "me"? Indeed, the very idea of living and working in community can be intimidating. The concept of intentional community asks us to look beyond that which we hold most dear, our own personal identities, to a larger, communal identity.

At the same time, though, being in community doesn't mean one must entirely lose oneself and one's identity. Rather, commitment to community is often the result of careful, self-reflective recognition of the strengths and limitations of one's own uniqueness. In its most healthy and functional iteration, a community can strengthen and empower its members to use their individual gifts to contribute to the community, to the Church, and to the world; a commitment to community also recognizes that we can most fully live into who God created us to be when we allow ourselves to depend on the strengths of others to help us in our own weaknesses.

At Saint Hilda's House, this reflective journey is embodied through the program's focus on discernment, the process of exploring the questions of who God is calling us to be and how God is calling us to live and work in the world. Interns are asked to live in the tension of the "me" and the "we" and explore these questions together. Saint Hilda's recognizes that learning to know oneself and learning to know God does not happen in a vacuum. We learn about ourselves, the world around us, and the Divine through interactions and relationships; at the same time, these interactions also create opportunities for us to help others learn and grow.

Of course, relationships are hard work. For all of the joys and benefits that come with building relationships with others, there are as many difficulties. To be in community, one must dwell in a precarious and vulnerable place, opening oneself to love, happiness, and rich relationship but also to being hurt or undervalued. Even under the best of circumstances, living and working in community is not an easy endeavor and comes with its share of struggles.

One can probably imagine that when a group of diverse strangers are brought together to live in community, conflict will ensue. Yet it may be surprising to know that one of the most common, perennial conflicts in Saint Hilda's House is over something very simple: washing dishes. You may never realize how much it bothers you to have dirty dishes in the sink until you have lived with someone who doesn't wash up after him- or herself, or may never realize how a roommate leaving dishes for you to wash might lead you to feel as though you and your time are not valued. Daily interactions with other members of a community teach us about our values, our preferences, and ourselves. These interactions may reinforce boundaries we knew we had or reveal to us boundaries we never imagined existed. They may chip away at our conceptions of our understanding of relationship, community, or even ourselves and God. In fact, all of these things will probably be challenged and maybe even changed.

Daily interactions with other members of a community teach us about our values, our preferences, and ourselves.

I find that one of the best analogies I can find for this project of communal living is to liken it to archeology. Over the course of several years, I had the opportunity to work with a group excavating a Civil War prison camp and spent many hours sifting through dirt as I looked for, excavated, and cleaned artifacts. As we worked, we used a series of intricate tools such as trowels and brushes.

The project of communal living and formation is a bit like this archeological process. As we live and work with others and seek to know and love God more fully, each interaction or experience we have is a brush or trowel, removing our dirt and debris, revealing what is underneath to us and to those we encounter. Sometimes what is uncovered is stunningly beautiful and sometimes what is uncovered is utterly broken. Yet no matter the condition of what is discovered, it always provides an opportunity to learn about the past and help inform the future.

Living in community is not simply about abandoning the self; living and working in community is about discovering who we are by allowing ourselves to be exposed and vulnerable, by continually reflecting on what we learn in the process, by allowing ourselves to be changed by the Holy Spirit and by the relationships we form.

Lex Orandi, Lex Credendi—*Aleithia Burgess*

It's January. I'm a doctoral student in Scotland, and I've been invited to present a paper at a conference in Chicago. Needing a place to stay, I contact a few friends, and one of them directs me to the Order of St. Anne, which has an Episcopal convent on the Near North Side. I'm not sure what to expect, but I'm looking forward to my visit. It's been a rough winter so far, and I'd love the chance for a little extra prayer and reflection.

The convent is located in a Victorian house next door to the very Anglo-Catholic Church of the Ascension. When I arrive, the sisters are out, but the housekeeper, a friendly woman with a strong Milwaukee accent, lets me in and offers me a cup of tea. I sit at the end of a long table, hands clasped around the mug for warmth, and drink in my surroundings. The building is gorgeous: high ceilings, dark woodwork, massive doors, and twisting staircase. The furnishings are well worn, though clearly cared for. The mantle and side tables are crowded with knickknacks, and yellowing pictures of angels and Bible verses hang on the walls. I'm struck by how much this place resembles the parochial house from the Irish sitcom *Father Ted*. However, set dressers had ironically selected Father Ted's kitschy décor. These objects, when they'd been put here half a century ago, genuinely had been thought to be in good taste. I do not laugh. The historian in me is intrigued; I've stepped into the past.

Before long, the sisters return. There are two: Sister Barbara, a sweet Chicagoan who's been with the Convent for decades, and Mother Judith, a short South Indian woman with a strong character. We begin with the usual small talk.

"What first brought you to Chicago, Mother Judith?" I ask.

"God brought me here," she tells me.

Sister Barbara wants to rest, so Mother Judith shows me around and explains their daily schedule. "We begin with Matins at 6:00 a.m. in the chapel, and at 6:40 we go over to the church for Morning Prayer, followed by Mass at 7."

"Is it okay if I join you?" I ask.

"Absolutely," she says.

The previous year, I'd lived in a different sort of intentional Christian community. We weren't particularly monastic; just a bunch of twenty-somethings trying to figure out what it means to actually live by Jesus's command to "love God, and love other people." One of our disciplines was reading Morning Prayer together (at the more sensible hour of 8:00 a.m.), and over time, it became very meaningful for me.

Having grown up in an evangelical church where "corporate prayer" meant that the associate pastor stood up and free-styled for five to ten minutes (as kids used to time him), I was intrigued by the concept of liturgy. When you read the same words day in and day out, you absorb them; they sink deep into your brain and blood and bones, and form a rhythm you can build your life upon. Through repetition, the words become *your* words, which you offer up to the God "in whom we live and move and have our being."

I'd had a copy of the prayer book for several years before I ever set foot in an Episcopal Church, but it was the "common" element that really brought liturgy to life for me. Praying together with others in my community taught me how we pray *for* one another, and I don't mean in the sense that we remind God about Sarah's job search or Daniel's grandfather's funeral (not that those things aren't important). What I mean is, when we pray together, we become the voice for those among us or absent from us who are too anguished or angry or weary or otherwise unable to speak for themselves. There were mornings when I showed up in the chapel and could do nothing but sit and listen and let my friends' words wash over me:

"Create in us clean hearts, O God;
And sustain us with thy Holy Spirit."

The next morning, just before six, a bell rings. The faint drone of psalms being spoken floats up through the floorboards. It's early for me, but I roll out of bed anyway and head for the shower. For the past four months, Morning Prayer, like pretty much everything else in my life, has been something that I do alone. I'm not about to miss the chance for company.

At six thirty-eight, I'm crossing the courtyard between the convent and the church. Snow is falling and the wind chill must be near zero (which really makes me regret having wet hair), but I make it in time. Sitting in the pews are Mother Judith, Sister Barbara, and a man who I assume is a parishioner. Father Williams, the interim rector, officiates. His reading voice is magnificent; and I find out later that he's a former Baptist, like me.

"Lord, open our lips;
And our mouth shall proclaim your praise."

We're using Rite Two rather than One, which is what I learned. I remember the debates, a few of them heated, that some people in our community had gotten into over this issue, and I smile. In the end, it's not really about the words we use, but the attitude that lies beneath them.

Even so, I find it comforting to know that on any given day, there are people all over the world who are praying the same prayers that I pray. Even if we pray alone, we are still praying together. Liturgy helps me remember that I am not alone in my faith, but am part of something much bigger than myself, something that stretches across space and time: the

I find it comforting to know that on any given day, there are people all over the world who are praying the same prayers that I pray.

Body of Christ. How else do we become part of that communion of saints but by being in community with those who are around us, here and now?

At the end of the week, I don't want to leave; not the country, the city, or the convent. Not because I want to become a nun—although Mother Judith tells me that in twenty years of being in the convent, I'm the first girl she's met whom she really thinks would be suited for the religious life. (This both flatters and frightens me.) Rather, being here has helped me to realize how much my life right now lacks community, which is what I want more than anything else. How do I face going back to being alone? I confide my anxieties to Mother Judith, and she gives me a big hug.

"Worry less, pray more," she tells me. "And remember, we're praying with you."

Giving Up Control—*Carrie Staab*

"We." That is the first word that comes to my mind when I think about this experience of living in community. I thought of it because, these days, it seems I can't get through a sentence without it.

It wormed its way into my speech early on, sneakily peppering my sentences. By the four-month mark of living in community, I found myself using it with a consistency and ferocity one associates only with royalty or newly smitten couples. My overdose on the plural pronoun eventually came to my awareness when a friend from outside the program (they exist, believe it or not) pointed it out in a somewhat exasperated tone, noting the stark change in my self-identification.

This friend knew me in high school and college, when I was very much an "I"—my goals, my talents, all done on my time according to my effort. It was all up to me, never mind those who sacrificed and worked hard to get me there in the first place! It was a comforting notion, as I alone knew what I could do. Where I went was up to me and ultimately I was in control of the process.

But God has a way of screwing up those comfortable little pictures of reality. While my reentry into Christianity initially brought with it the easy and nice things that faith could provide, eventually

I entered the community at Saint Hilda's and had to learn, am still learning, the difficulties of faith—the hard work of loving, serving, and working with God's people. It became clear to me that in the end, it wasn't about me; it's not just my goals at stake, my talents alone that achieve them, nor is it done on my timeline.

Believe me on that one—it's not done on my timeline. This was the first lesson, and one of the most important to me, because it involves giving up so much of the control I was accustomed to having. Waiting, I believe, is one of the most humiliating experiences for me (to be totally at the mercy of someone else who *won't hurry up!*), and seems to turn me into the worst version of myself: selfish, antsy, anxious. It strips me bare and brings out the parts of me that I wish others could never see.

This frustrating process of waiting is something that is essential in community. On a practical level, there are the logistics to consider of coordinating the schedules and habits of eleven people, resulting in what we call the "Hildan Shuffle," that awkward ten to twenty minute period when some house members are sitting in the foyer, ready to go, and others are searching for jackets, shoes, cell phones, etc. After enough times, though, we accepted this as inevitable, and the bench and two stools in our foyer have become another place of interaction for those who wait; I have started to embrace the time spent there (mostly).

Beyond that, though, there is something a bit more difficult to define: the ability to wait on a person. After wondering why some people rarely responded when I talked to them, I learned to stop at the end of my sentences, take a big breath, and wait; sooner or later, a response will come, on their own time. Eventually, I thought to do the same at the end of *their* sentences; giving myself space to reflect on what they said, and not jumping in with an answer I'd formulated halfway through their first sentence, but really *listening*. In not wanting to control the person I was interacting with, I had to give up the ability to dictate the nature and pace of our interactions. I had to make space for them in my life by giving up some of what I wanted. Sometimes this means slowing down when you walk, or sitting quietly instead of talking, or watching a truly terrible movie for the sake of someone else.

However, going too far in either direction is dangerous.

Community can be addicting; the closeness can be overwhelming. The desire to be with everyone all the time, to be available every moment of the day, leads to burnout pretty quickly. The times I have felt most frustrated in community are when I had to give up so much of myself that I didn't know where in the group I belonged. I had to learn that sometimes being a blessing to others meant removing myself, taking time to do things that mattered to me. If I gave up too much of myself to the group, there eventually wouldn't be any left to give—community burnout, complete assimilation, driven up the wall by the slowness of group processing and community life. Just as I'm no good to the community if I think of only myself, I'm no good if I think only of others; I need to be me, but me in relation to that group.

I lost some control of my life, let others have a say in it, let them determine the pace and nature of my days. In doing so, I became part of a group, a larger we, a process that helps me learn to accept God's presence in my life. Making yourself vulnerable to other people ups the ante of your faith, makes certain that your promises Sunday morning in church are held throughout the week, and gives you the strength to do so. None of this happens without giving up control. Not all of it, but some of it—enough to allow room for others in your life, enough to balance your needs with theirs, your emotions with theirs. Giving up too much leads to you being swallowed whole and feeling lost.

Making yourself vulnerable to other people ups the ante of your faith,

As I slowly work out what my vocation is, this patience and trust is integral. I spent a lot of time asking questions and worrying about the uncertainty, but I've started to learn to stop, take a breath, and wait for the response on a time that is not entirely my own.

Confidence and Clarification—*Ardath Dixon*

I came to Saint Hilda's House with some knowledge on group process and intentional communities, after facilitating group bonding week after week in New Hampshire the previous year. I had been lit up, so to speak, empowered from living in a beautiful safe haven for a year. I felt ready to enter "the real world" and live among the brutal honesty in society. Saint Hilda's began with a fair amount of challenges, and I felt ready. They fell into the category of what I call "type two fun," difficult in the moment and entertaining afterward. I share a room barely large enough for two twin beds? Ha, at least it's bigger than the tent I shared last summer. I spend days sorting books alone? Ha, at least fellow service members are doing similar odd work at other schools. The kids I tutor have difficult behavior? Ha, at least they will be the same students all year, so I'll get through to them one way or another. My housemates don't get along? Ha, this is our group's "storming" phase as I learned from camp; it would all turn out for the good.

My year of Saint Hilda's House began around the same time as the Occupy movement. Being the young, liberal, curious Christians we were, a few of us decided to bring candles and leaflets to lead a Compline service on the New Haven Green amidst the Occupiers. The first time we did so, we used a mic check with repeats and picked up a few curious strangers. We gave candles to those present, and shared the psalms and creeds that are so engrained in my mind. This was the type of church I had come to crave when living in remote New Hampshire; a community that is honest, kind, open, and present alongside the challenges of society.

Following the service, four of us walked back toward the church with our candles lit, and we started singing. If someone's candle blew out, another helped relight it. I have frequently considered the metaphor of being a candle amidst the darkness. Having been strengthened in an incredibly supportive community, alongside its roaring fire, I could bring light and hope into other areas of darkness. I had experienced this process several times before arriving in New Haven. For instance, a semester abroad living in community and studying natural beauty reenergized me so that I could empower my teammates back at my home campus in the states. That following summer, I discovered that I could encourage fellow political canvassers to remain optimistic after being frequently dismissed by pedestrians. It was my responsibility to bring this hope, this support, and this love to those who were struggling. However, I had also found that if my surroundings proved to be too much, too strong or too windy, my strength and hope could be blown out. I lived with the understanding that to become rekindled, I would need to completely immerse myself in a supportive, caring community again—another roaring fire.

When arriving in New Haven for a year of social work, I believed that once again, I was to be a candle in the darkness. However, as we all walked toward the church with four flickering candles, I was reminded that I don't need to be alone. I do not have to solve the problems of this world alone, solely with strength fed to me from God. As we walked, each candle did blow out at some point. However, others' surrounding flames enabled us all to relight each other and continue walking through the dark wind. This taught me how I do not need to choose between being a single flickering candle and living in a flaming room of light. I can bring light to traverse the darkness, the chaos of our reality, and be alongside others who can relight me and whom I can relight if blown out. I discovered that I could trust my peers, colleagues, and housemates for support and encouragement if I started to flicker.

Strong communal support plus daily, intense, relevant challenging environments was a new pairing revealed to me at Saint Hilda's House. I also found strong peer religious dialogue, which was fascinating. I was no longer "the religious one" in my group of friends, no longer the one who said, "Oh my gosh," nor the one who was busy Sunday mornings. In fact, housemates lovingly teased me for being as Protestant as you can get! I discovered a sense of freedom in the continuity that flowed throughout the Saint Hilda's lifestyle. Rather than hopping between different groups of people for different activities, I attended church services with the same people whom I would have dance parties with, who were the same people I lived with, all sharing similar work environments. Saint Hilda's House helped me clarify aspects of my personal faith. I learned the difference between Rite I and Rite II in the Book of Common Prayer. I witnessed a range of preferences regarding prayer, whether prewritten or spontaneous, whether spoken or sung. I found deeper understanding regarding the debate between holding fast to tradition or changing with the times, and how they can take shape in a wide variety of ways throughout churches.

Theologically, Saint Hilda's House gave me a newfound confidence in my faith, since I constantly witnessed liberal openness paired with strong devotion to God. Prior to Saint Hilda's House, I felt a sense of tension between Church practices, societal relevance, and open support. While I had previously seen friction regarding homosexuality in the Church, this was no issue whatsoever in our program. Multiple priests, housemates, and friends were both gay and Christian leaders. We lived the conservative liturgy of Rite I Morning Prayer with the liberal theology of open doors to all. This again was freeing! I did not have to defend Christianity with liberal agnostic friends, nor petition for gay rights among conservative Christian friends. Rather, frequent theology in our house held the "both and" mentality. We could laugh about certain nuances of our faiths and live with a sense of trust. The year freed me from feeling responsible to defend Christianity as an entire system. I could finally watch disturbing footage of intense conservatives across our nation and not feel ashamed. I could discuss these beliefs with friends who grew up as the liberal minority in environments such as Missouri and Alabama, the polar opposite from myself in Massachusetts. I discovered a deeper sense of patience. Rather than feeling anger toward loud, conservative Christians who "give us a bad name," as I often had said, I came to understand how much of their theology is based in fear.

At camp the previous year, I learned this tension as it applies to youth development, whether using fear as motivation or using tools that inspire empowerment. I saw lasting growth from positive, loving facilitation. Fear could yield immediate changes, but these would come out of spite or anger. Living in Christian community inspired me to apply this lesson to the Church at a deeper level, recognizing God to be defined by love. Similar to behavior management where students are told to obey or be suspended, some see the theological choice as obedience to God or eternal suffering in hell. However, the youth development strategy from camp used loving dialogue to help with behavior. Leaders would honestly ask the student what was going on, learn the cause, and collaborate to result in more lasting behavior changes. Students adjusted their behavior out of a desire to take ownership and grow, not out of a desire to immediately avoid the big, mean adult.

I found that this loving, present dialogue corresponds with the life of Jesus. The story of the flood in Genesis and laws found in Leviticus demonstrated one leadership strategy, but then God came down to earth to lovingly connect and inspire humanity on our own level. Jesus's teachings, miracles, brutal suffering, and Easter victory show how love conquers all. God is love. Likewise, our service work needed to be based on love. We could not scare someone into getting a job, obtaining food, or finding a place to live. We were there to help serve those in need, aspiring toward the loving selflessness of Jesus.

This unassuming, consistent, present love taught me a new-found patience for daily challenges in our house and at my worksite. To begin with, I witnessed a range of personality types and confrontation strategies. Living in close quarters with seven others, and repeatedly seeing eight more, showed me exactly how different personalities could interact. I learned how to connect more deeply with others, whether housemates or faculty, and how to encourage dialogue among peers. I learned how precisely to get responses from the principal and faculty at the K-8 public school where I worked. I learned that strong statements from loud personalities could be less entrenched, as opposed to the less frequent and more intentional statements from quieter personalities. At the same time, I came to recognize a difference between simple acceptance ("it is what it is") and inspirational growth. The serenity prayer articulates this quite well with the words, "God, grant me the serenity to accept the things I cannot change, the courage to change the things I can, and wisdom to know the difference." I discovered how my input could indeed positively impact house meetings, chore rotations, and group dynamics. I could take my lessons from camp to encourage dialogue and positive group development within our house. Meanwhile, I was comforted by the fact that it was not solely my responsibility to make it work. I was alongside equals in our house, and I could help; yet it was not my downfall if things did not work out perfectly. I constantly reminded myself that the first step is love, and the rest will follow.

Saint Hilda's House gave me a newfound confidence with all aspects of my personality, while teaching a greater sense of patience and acceptance. My faith, my athleticism, my love for strong communities, my New England upbringing, and my public school involvement all became united and intertwined. I found reassurance with my faith in a house where anything and everything was honest and present. I rediscovered value in speaking my mind, whether from house meetings or from psalms with verses like "I cry to the Lord with my voice; to the Lord I make loud supplication. I pour out my complaint before him and tell him all my trouble" (142:1–2). I discerned that I have a deeper care for strong communities than your typical adult, as well as the realization that if I am alone, everyone else is not necessarily doing something fun without me. I found freedom in a theology based solely on love, and witnessed the societal response it attracted from its openness to all. I learned deeper patience to meeting people where they are, and with that, I discovered freedom to put my honest self and opinions out there. Saint Hilda's House shared with me a new sense of stability, service, camaraderie, humility, and courage.

Finding Myself—*Jessa Fowler*

It's really not that far from New York City to New Haven, Connecticut, but to do it for the first time, after a full day of rerouted flights, on two hours of sleep, and all your worldly possessions divided between a gigantic backpack and a cardboard box, seemed pretty impossible. I braced myself for the bus, the train, and the taxi ride I'd need to figure out as I touched down at JFK. I'll never forget the pings of the most beautiful text messages I'd ever seen come in as I turned my phone on. *Hi, we're from Saint Hilda's House. Hi, we heard you need a ride. Hi, don't worry—we're coming to get you.* I knew, from the moment we settled my bags around the six people that had crammed into the minivan that had come to my rescue, that I was beginning one of the most unique and unforgettable experiences of my life. It wasn't until later, though, that I realized the impact that this community would have on me, as an individual.

I've found it pretty easy on the street, at work, or even among friends, to be kind, considerate, and loving. It's not hard to hold the door for a stranger, to give your change to someone on the street who needs it, to buy a birthday present for a friend, and then go about your day as normal. I have a tendency to live this kind of life and to keep people at a cordial arm's length. To keep people on the periphery, I could avoid getting enmeshed in the brokenness of humanity.

Living in community, I couldn't choose to interact with people on my terms, when I wanted to, or when I felt up to it. The nature of our program—living, worshiping, working, and eating together—created a foundation of shared experience, values, and expectations that intensified our interactions with one another. By waking up early to pray together, spending Saturday mornings on house grocery trips, or sharing an evening meal together, I found my shell, my hesitancy to live authentically and vulnerably, stripped away.

What was left was a new understanding of how my actions as an individual shaped my relationships. By making small sacrifices, taking the time to smile at someone who was struggling, asking someone to go for a walk, or simply spending time sitting and talking, I began to build the kind of relationships I think that Jesus called us to have when he said love your neighbor as yourself. As I got to know my housemates, I learned that "loving my neighbor" looked different for different people. And as I learned more about the quirks and idiosyncrasies of the group, this diversity of people gave me opportunity to feel comfortable expressing myself, to learn new things and develop new interests, and make life-long friends.

> As I got to know my housemates, I learned that "loving my neighbor" looked different for different people.

Some of what was surprising to me about this was that it was not just what I choose to do, but also what I choose not to do that mattered. By thinking only of myself—leaving a mess in the sink or music on late at night—I learned how my actions might affect others without me even realizing it. By missing things like Morning Prayer or community meetings, I personally lost out in the richness in participating in community life, but more importantly, my absence left a tangible void within the community.

Even as I learned new lessons in accountability and the importance of community norms, I found the need for grace and flexibility, to accommodate for the things that just come up in life. Living in community pushed me to act in love even when I was frustrated, tired, or just wanted to be alone. I learned the importance of dropping what I wanted or was doing to comfort a friend in need. And by living this way, I never knew which one of my housemates would be there to do the same for me, but I knew that there would be someone.

And then, somewhere in the middle of the daily events of community life—work crises, Friday night dinners, homesickness, and birthday celebrations, I realized I was finding my identity in the midst of community. As issues came up, I was challenged to think for myself, and not drift with the group's majority opinion. It also didn't take me long to realize there was a reason that Jesus took off sometimes to sit quietly with God, and that sometimes I needed to do the same thing and take time alone, to take care of myself.

But as enlightening and restful as the solitude can be, I think there's a reason we aren't called to be hermits, a reason that Jesus always comes back down from the mountain. I wouldn't trade the trials and tribulations that I experienced in my Saint Hilda's community in a billion years because with these came some of the most joyful and loving relationships I've ever had. And by building relationships with others in community, with both the ups and the downs, I was able to become more of who I am and live more fully into the abundant life that Christ promises.

Interdependence—*James Shire*

When I was living in China, I had a conversation with a certain taxi driver. He said that despite the increasing wealth and prosperity of China, he would rather live in the China under Mao Tse-tung. He acknowledged the poverty and the challenges of living under Mao's regime, but what was important to him was that during those years he knew that if his home were to burn down, his neighbors would not only help to put out the fire, but they would help him recover from it as well. These days, in modern China, there is no such help from neighbors. This seems like an oddly paradoxical thing; there is more wealth in China now than ever, there is a growing middle class, and their national economic situation is healthier than anywhere in the world. In many ways, China, though a market socialist economy, has a thriving capitalistic-style economy that seemingly outpaces the American economy. And yet, here is someone who thinks it was better under Mao.

I never fully grasped this paradox until I had an opportunity to live within an intentional community.

In our lives, we have these communal moments or instances. We find them in our parishes, our places of employment, and our schools, to name a few. There is a certain sense of shared life for these short periods, and then we return to our individual existences. We are individuals; we desire and cherish our autonomy and independence. We extoll self-sufficiency. We only need to care for ourselves. We do not need to depend upon our neighbors to help us. We go to our classes, jobs, and church services. We know and are friendly with many people and make polite conversation with others. However, we dare not be honest and disclose any negativity when someone asks, "How are you doing?" lest we reveal our needs and vulnerabilities and therefore risk dependency. We have our friends who we can be open with, but these too are isolated instances. More often than not, we find ourselves alone and by ourselves for many hours. Even in urban settings where millions of people are packed into a small geographical location, how many people actually know their neighbors?

It is here where I realize what the taxi driver said had some truth to it. Despite our wealth and self-sufficiency, our independence reveals our isolation.

For me what is most tragic is that our Christian reality is caught in this. We have a sense of community together in our churches and parishes. But how much do we share in each other's lives? Christian life historically has always been punctuated by community life with the practices of monasticism and the confraternities of Roman Catholicism. However, it seems in the American Christian experience, these are the exceptions, not the norm. Instead, we have embraced a message of individual salvation through Jesus Christ, seemingly treating all else as secondary.

When I was living within an intentional community, a community where we agreed to live together, work together, and share a common prayer life together, I began to realize how flawed our individualistic model of living is. Particularly as Christians, though some are called to a life of isolated asceticism, most of our lives ought to be defined as communal. We believe in a communal God within the Trinity, we believe in Jesus Christ who was surrounded by his closest disciples and apostles, and we believe we are a continuation of those first communities in Acts. And in my community, I recognized a way to live with Christ that was never articulated before.

One of the things that I learned was that it is okay to be vulnerable with others and dependent on other people. In my opinion, I think some people, myself included, all too often shut others out of our spaces and lives, only inviting them to cross the border on our specific terms. In community, we begin to recognize that those borders are fuzzy, and sometimes nonexistent, and in this we are liberated from our isolation; we recognize that we have to help one another and care for one another, especially when our houses are "on fire."

In community, where we share our lives together, we begin to be able to look at ourselves in the mirror of the eyes of others in our community and begin to recognize just who we are because when we live with others in the mundane rotations of life, we see where we are strongest, and where we need to grow most. We learn from one another, we shape one another, and we begin to blend with one another to help us grow into new people. This is especially true in our communal lives as Christians. In our common prayer, we recognize the needs of one another because we are living intimately with one another. We can pray with each other in ways that we would not conceive of on our own because we can ask one another, "How are you?" and answer honestly. It is not always perfect, conflicts can arise, differences in habits and lifestyle can become sources of argument, and there are always dirty dishes, but despite that, or perhaps because of it, we learn to live with and grow with one another.

I think that the idea of communal living, community, or other variants of this are floating around in American Christianity as an alternative to the individual trend of our Christian experience. If we are called to a life with Christ, I believe on some level we surrender our autonomy not only so that we can be in community with the Triune God, but also with one another. We are the Body of Christ. That means we have to be on some level connected to one another and sharing with one another, as we are one body. It is through living in community that we begin to recognize that we are that one body.

Communal Transformation—*Rick Durance*

I remember sitting in one of my favorite sandwich shops with a Lutheran pastor during college. I had been attending services at her church and the local Episcopal campus ministry for over a year. While regularly attending services and events at both of these places, I found some of my closest college friends and a way to balance life at college. After years of trying to disengage from the church, I found myself seriously contemplating self-identifying unconditionally as Christian again. Yet on that day, in that restaurant, I tried to leave it all because of how strange I found this new life. I had begun to do these weird church things and, worse still, believe some pretty ridiculous Christian stuff again. I blamed her along with a cohort of other religious people for warping my mind for their own purposes. I told her I was leaving and I needed her to be all right with that.

Without missing a beat, she said that it was not they who were changing me. It was not some conspiracy to brainwash me into believing something. What I was panicking about was part of a larger transformation. She reminded me that Christ calls us into new and unending life. What I was experiencing was the essence of the Christian faith. All of this was Jesus stuff at its best.

Looking back after spending five years with these varied types of intentional religious communities, I can testify that these places, from campus ministries to religious service years, will transform you. Especially after a very intense year with the Saint Hilda's Episcopal Service Corp site, living into these lives changes you. These communities will help turn you into who you really are. I would not have been able to compassionately listen to those I served on a crisis line in San Francisco without this other-focused faith that has grown around me. They have helped me to see the truth about this human experience and the importance of Christian service. I could not continue working at my soup kitchen worksite if I did not experience something cosmically significant in the simple act of providing someone with a meal for that day.

> These communities will help turn you into who you really are.

These community-driven transformations have connected me deeply with God by forcing me to face and live into what it true. While living in Saint Hilda's House, it has been easy to project specific beliefs or other expectations on my housemates. Yet my community checks these illusions. When a housemate can bring you to tears through impromptu and unscripted grace at dinner, there has to be enormous significance in the radical spontaneity often missing from my life. Although scripture and our tradition might contain all that is necessary for salvation, Christ's work is not limited. Community teaches how to see Jesus and your own salvation within our Christian and secular lives together. By connecting to reality through others, we participate in the larger story of the Incarnation. We become Christ for each in quite a tangible way. I have had the bittersweet joy of being present as housemates grieve for family members, while they have been there for me through a quiet embrace and talk through homesickness. We quite literally embody Jesus as well as our full unpretentious selves for each other.

This participation in the divine through others is not easy. Even after years of this lifestyle, it still makes me uncomfortable. Every couple months, I have still found myself blurting out to fellow members of Saint Hilda's that "I just want to be normal" or "It is just not worth staying here anymore." Yet that next day or the next week, I am back at Morning Prayer or a house dinner. I am still not sure why that happens. I do not know how I still continue directing my life toward prayer or service much less this ministry of staying for my all brothers and sisters in Christ. I can only say it is not me. It has to be grace from God in the form of these people in my life. These moments are outward manifestations of what we call "Church" and demonstrate how these communities are significant to the Christian faith.

Therefore, I believe these communities are among the most necessary endeavors that we can embark on for both ourselves and for Body of Christ in the world. One of the most profound realities that these communities reveal is that the Church is more than bells, beliefs, or buildings. It is us. We are the Church when we ask each other to pray for us during the week, make food for someone who is having a rough time, sit with each other through worship, donate our time at local food banks, or show up on the steps of the Capital to assure our neighborhood's food security. They are a reminder both to us as individuals and as society that Church is not a narrow once-a-week or personal activity. It is your life among others.

The significance of these places and the communal

transformations they cultivate means a lot for the Church at large. If I can find a way to face my own demons of cynicism and the deep-rooted mistrust, then what could we as the Church find? I hope that if the Church can provide a true sense of home for me, then hopefully it can do the same for others. By developing ourselves and our local communities to be prepared to be Christ for each other, then we become piece by piece a holy, catholic, and apostolic church.

Reflection Questions

■ What have been the most life-giving and affirming communities you have lived or participated in? What made them so?

■ What is the difference between experiencing community prayer and personal prayer?

■ How do you make space for the voice and habits of others?

■ Reflect upon Carrie Staab's statement, "Making yourself vulnerable to other people ups the ante of your faith."

■ When have you experienced (or given) a candle amidst the darkness?

■ What does James Shire mean by "Despite our wealth and self-sufficiency, our independences reveals our isolation."

CHAPTER 10

Communities Changing
the Church

Imagine a Church

WHEN WE BEGAN SAINT HILDA'S House, our notion was that a life of regular prayer, service, and worship would change the young people joining the community here. Like so many churches and institutions, we perhaps spent less time thinking about how they would change us. But watching the young adults who have come through the program and parish one cannot help but be heartened and full of hope about how they might call the Church into new life. As we welcome them into our midst, we know that there is an experience of the holy here that can transform those who enter into it and draw them closer to Christ. Yet they too are calling us closer to Christ as well.

The people coming out of Saint Hilda's and communities like it will be, quite simply, some of the finest leaders both lay and ordained that the Church will see. They will be formed in what it means to live as Christians. Prayer, openness to change, healthy vulnerability, an awareness of others, an engagement with theology and tradition, a knowledge of the challenges of our wider communities, and a commitment to live beyond themselves are all part of their life here and I can't imagine a finer way to prepare people for a life of witness to the gospel.

Imagine a vestry with just one or two young adults that have been formed in this way serving on it. Imagine someone entering seminary with this kind of preparation. Imagine a nurse who has lived in this way. Imagine a social worker that has lived in this kind of community. No matter the field that these young adults enter, they will be grounded in the essentials of the faith that will give them a way to express how they see God at work around them. They will be our finest evangelists, our most eloquent preachers, and our frontline theologians, for they will have embodied the essence of sacrificial and prayerful Christian living.

These young adults will be the conscience of our Church and can restore our sense of obligation to make known the Good News. A life in community is necessarily a life of Good News. They spend a year or more sharing in such a way that they become fluent in the language of faith. Their work of evangelism will not be the fumbling, crude thing that often marks too many evangelical efforts. They will have been changed and that change will mark them as something slightly different—someone worth knowing a little better. Their experiences will give them the confidence to offer testimony to the power of forgiveness and witness to the grace of love.

When I lived in the Deep South and was a Roman Catholic, my then girlfriend (now wife) and I mostly attended a Roman Catholic Church. When my wife was working in a local gift shop as we paid our way through school, she was asked where she went to church—and she told them. The customer paid, left the store, and then returned to inform my wife that God had spoken to her about my wife's soul and that she needed to leave the false church we had been attending. Another person once, in all honesty, asked why I was attending a church that "worshiped a dead woman." As you might imagine, experiences like this did little to advance the gospel these folks were committed to sharing with us.

Imagine a different way of evangelism—an evangelism rooted in transformed people living lives of faith that radiate change, newness, and holiness. I am not talking about Hallmark holiness—the kind that is hazy and filled with softly lit cherubs. I am talking of the kind of holiness that holds dying hands, that walks with those who limp, that reads with those without sight, that feeds those who hunger—I am talking of a holiness of life that can only change the whole Church around it. I believe this is the great promise of communities like these—they prepare young people to be more authentically Christian and they will call the Church into newness of life.

These young adults are a living catechesis—they are teaching all of us how to be more fully Christian. Through faithful study, disciplined prayer, self-giving, honest relationships, and more, they are patterning what a life of service and witness looks like. Just as they are changed they will, if we dare to let them, change us for the better. They are not joining these communities or even the Church as a whole out of a sense of social obligation or as a hobby—they are coming and asking to be transformed. By sharing all that we have to offer with integrity and energy, we will be laying the ground for a living, breathing, and thriving Church to emerge—a Church that brims with holiness.

The work of holiness is the casting aside of those measures of the self that have previously allowed for the luxury of a purely personal God who asks little of us and changes us not a whit—a God whose silence is deafening, because to truly hear would be to be undone as so-called self-made men and women. God is calling us to deeper relationship with him and for us to cast aside things, behaviors, and routines that impede that relationship. This is the truly radical challenge of the whole narrative of the biblical witness—God is always calling us to deeper relationship. These communities are a chance to explore what it actually means to be in relationship both with one another and with God—they are an opportunity to discover anew what it means to be people of God sharing the gifts of God.

The Presence of Young Adults—*Jordan Trumble*

When I first made the decision to spend time living in intentional community, many people in my life approved of my decision and offered me support, but I also had a few people who treated me as though I was a little crazy. When I described to one friend that I would be living in community at a church, he replied, "So you're basically going to be a nun for a year?" This question made me wonder: when did living a life of faith that is grounded in community become so strange?

As human beings, we are inherently relational creatures; we are sons or daughters and grandchildren, and many of us are also parents and siblings. Most of us go by names that have been handed down from other family members, making our own names badges of our membership in particular family communities. We often define even our understanding of how we exist with God by this relational language: we are God's children, created in God's own image. Our identities are inextricably entwined with the identities of others and of God.

> *When did living a life of faith that is grounded in community become so strange?*

At the very basis of our theology, too, is an affirmation of the importance of community; each time we say the creed, we are professing a belief in a Triune God whose own self offers us an example of community and relationship. And so, again, I must ask the question: when did living a life of faith that is grounded in community become so strange?

Since the beginning of Christianity, followers of Christ have been gathering or living in community, from small groups of early desert monastics and the monastic orders of the Middle Ages to the modern-day Catholic Worker Mmvement and dozens of faith-based young adult internship programs around the country and world. The project of Saint Hilda's House and other similar programs isn't an entirely new concept; it is merely a new iteration of one of the core values of Christianity: community. As I have lived in community and studied community, though, one thing has become abundantly clear; although being in relationship is certainly part of the calling of the Christian life, living in intentional community is a particular calling that is not shared by all and is only one expression of a deeply authentic spiritual life.

While I understand that all do not share this calling to life in intentional community, I must emphatically assert that it is still an essential part of the modern Church. Intentional community is necessary to the modern Church because it achieves something we often fail to do—be simultaneously timely and timeless, to engage tradition without being traditional. This may seem incongruous, but it is really quite simple: intentional communities offer space for young adults to explore deeply burning questions of ultimacy in the midst of a culture that doesn't have the attention span to even finish asking all of those questions, let alone answer them.

Intentional communities like Saint Hilda's House only work and thrive because young adults are asking the questions of who God is calling them to be and how God is calling them to live in the world, and they are looking for a place where they can explore those questions with others. Programs like Saint Hilda's House only work and thrive because they are not prescriptive but rather have arisen as an answer to a deep spiritual need. Indeed, the proof is in the numbers: in 2009, Episcopal Service Corps had programs in six cities; in 2012, it had programs in more than twenty, and each year there are more applicants than spots in the programs.

Furthermore, these programs continue to thrive thanks to a firm grounding in Christian tradition that asks young adults to think about more than their own lives; young adults are asked to think about the working of God in the world and the lives and witnesses of generations. These communities ask their members to read, mark, and inwardly digest, but then to use this as fuel to live out their callings in the broader world. Without this tradition that guides, shapes, and inspires new expressions of faith, these intentional communities would be nothing more than groups of young adults sitting around talking about their feelings.

While one of the greatest gifts of young adult intentional communities is the work they do as venues for bringing young adults into the church and for young adults already in the church to engage their faith questions more deeply, the greatest thing that young adult communities can do for the broader church is to be a model of successful ministry. Young adult communities are thriving and flourishing because they have found a way of being both timely and timeless and of engaging tradition without necessarily being traditional, something all ministries of the Church and even the Church itself must do to survive.

Loving Our Neighbors—*Sarah Dunn*

When I graduated from college and began applying for Episcopal Service Corps programs, I was unaware of just how life-changing such an opportunity would be for me. At the time, while I was participating in the discernment process and preparing for seminary, I believed that the Episcopal Service Corps would serve as a "gap year." I was excited to take part in a year of service, living in intentional community, and worshipping my Lord, but I did not realize the impact such an experience would have on me. I could not imagine how my own sense of self and my potential leadership within the Church, as well as my outlook for the future of the Church, would be so altered by my time as a member of Saint Hilda's House in New Haven, Connecticut.

Upon my arrival to Saint Hilda's House, I was honestly taken aback by the neighborhood in which I would be living. It was most definitely unlike any of the neighborhoods in which I had grown up. The Hill neighborhood in New Haven isn't white, it isn't middle class, it's not well-kept, and it completely took me out of my comfort zone. I imagined myself doing ministry and had already done ministry in a neighborhood such as the Hill, but I never imagined myself actually living in such a place. Yet until this experience, I never really understood what Jesus meant when he said, "and love your neighbor as yourself."

As a resident of the Hill, my neighbors were no longer soccer moms, engineers, military officers, businesswomen, or classmates from school. But instead my neighbors consisted of the drug dealer a few doors down, the schizophrenic woman who threatened to call the cops on me, and the Portuguese couple who couldn't speak much English—except for a few consistently overused profanities. These people were the neighbors God had asked me to love, neighbors who were not very easy to love. But until I had met these people—my crazy, kooky, bless their souls neighbors—I had never really experienced the gospel of radical love. Jesus asks us to love those who are so inherently different from ourselves, with whom there is no connection, no semblance of similarity, except that they are children of God just as we are. They, and we all, are beloved children of God.

Looking forward into a future of ordained ministry, I know now that my love, and the love of my congregation, must extend past our parish walls. For our neighbors are not just the people sitting next to us in the pew, the people who are easy to love, but our neighbors are the undocumented immigrant working at the local restaurant, the addict who has been in and out of rehab over nine times, and the pedophile out on probation. Loving our neighbors as ourselves should be one of the most difficult and most uncomfortable things we ever do as Christians. Ever heard of tough love? Well, the radical love of the gospel is true definition of tough love. But even so, Jesus calls us to enter into relationship with our fellow human beings and commands us to love them as ourselves.

> *Loving our neighbors as ourselves should be one of the most difficult and most uncomfortable things we ever do as Christians.*

My year in the Episcopal Service Corps transformed the way I love my neighbor. Every person, no matter her lot in life, is fully deserving of my and God's love. I can only imagine how the Episcopal Church would change if it more fully encompassed Christ's command to radically love one's neighbor. Perhaps we would see an explosion of Latino/Hispanic ministries, serving the fastest growing ethnicity in the United States. Perhaps we would see a demographic shift in our congregations, to include those who do not possess any form of higher education. Perhaps we would see a community in conversation with fundamentalist Christians. Perhaps we would see a Eucharistic celebration that offers grape juice along with wine for those seeking sobriety. Perhaps we would see the realization of God's kingdom on earth.

In seminary, I consistently hear that the Episcopal Church is shrinking, drowning, dying. I am told to be afraid for the future of our church, that unless we change, we will not be around much longer. Yet in my opinion, we know what it takes to survive; we know that if we truly love God and our neighbors as ourselves, then we will not die, but thrive! The change the Episcopal Church is seeking is a reorientation toward the gospel of radical love. The realization of this love is not only life-changing for an individual, but is also life-changing for the Church.

Reflection Questions

■ *How do young adults teach the Church (and us) how to be more fully Christian?*

■ *Jordan Trumble writes, "Intentional community is necessary to the modern Church because it achieves something we often fail to do—be simultaneously timely and timeless, to engage tradition without being traditional." Do you agree? Disagree? Why?*

■ *What makes a young adult community in the Church thrive and flourish? What are the core elements needed?*

■ *What is radical love?*

True Religion

ONE OF MY FAVORITE COLLECTS in the Book of Common Prayer is from the Sunday closest to August 31st. It includes the wonderful line, "Graft in our hearts the love of thy Name: increase in us true religion."[16] The heart of Christian communities like Saint Hilda's House is the deepening of true religion. Of course, in our modern parlance, true religion more often refers to a brand of jeans rather than a deep and abiding faith—yet it is a term worth the reclaiming. It is true religion that will be the hope and promise of the Church of the coming decades. These communities, communities of true religion, reveal more about each of us so that more of Christ can be revealed in us—so that we become more deeply aware of the ways in which we fall short of Christ's example and the ways in which we are most joyfully revealing his love.

These communities create both a safe and a challenging space in which a Christian can more deeply know how God is calling them. When that work is engaged with honesty and healthy vulnerability, we are able to open ourselves not only to others but also to the transforming work of the Spirit in our lives. It is tempting to think that spirituality is a privately held notion—yet nothing can be further from the truth. Intentional communities create, on a small and

---

[16] Book of Common Prayer, Proper 17, p. 181.

intense scale, a model for how the Church can develop spirituality at its best. It supports, challenges, reveals, forms, and sends out its members to seek and serve Christ. It only functions when it is a place of authentic engagement and mindful awareness of others and of the deep bonds between us in those Spirit-filled places we call difference.

While at seminary, there was a group of us sitting around a table and somehow the topic of competition came up. Many around the table said things like, "Oh, I'm pretty competitive" or "I've never really been that competitive" and there were nods and affirmations. I, in all honesty, said, "I've never really been that competitive." The table erupted in laughter. I had not intended it as a joke! In all honesty, I had never thought of myself as competitive. That moment, and that honesty in that community, helped me to understand how my actions might be impacting others and how I was bringing a way of being from my past work into a setting in which it was, at best, incongruous, and at worst deleterious to my relationships with classmates. If the community had just been about niceness or about ease for the sake of getting along, there would have been no growth and no genuine relationships. Community rejects the cult of niceness and exorcises the demons of ease as it gets to the heart of true religion.

It is amazing what a group of fellow Christians can teach us about ourselves. We develop blind spots in which pieces of our past drive up behind us and just coast there in our wake. Community is that side mirror that announces, "Objects in mirror are closer than they appear." Those things that may have been a blind spot are right there and if we hit a bump or tap on the brake, we might find ourselves in an ugly collision. The same is true of our Church—young adults and communities of service are revealing the blind spots of the Church and calling us to more authentically Christian ways of being.

young adults and communities of service are revealing the blind spots of the Church and calling us to more authentically Christian ways of being.

Religion has something of a bad name now—we have lots of "nones" and "spiritual not religious" types floating around. It is my belief that they simply haven't encountered true religion—the kind being lived out in communities like Saint Hilda's. Religion is simply spirituality with consequences.

There is a kind of religion that washes feet, that carries crosses, that comforts the brokenhearted, that forgives, teaches, and heals. Communities like Saint Hilda's and parishes like Christ Church are places where that kind, that deeper kind, that authentic kind of religion might be found—a place where spirituality has consequences. When one joins a community, takes on a rigorous life of prayer, commits to a worship that demands much, delves ever deeper into a shared identity, it will have deep and lasting consequences for you and for all those with whom you are in relationship.

This kind of religion is always revealing who we are and who we are meant to be as we are drawn more deeply into the life of the community. Our identity acquires a relational shape. Each of us knows ourselves by our relationships—this is a good and healthy thing when our sense of self is known in the context of how we love, share, and nurture. It becomes an unhealthy thing when we define ourselves by how ground down we are by the demands of the community or any relationship. God asks us to be living sacrifices—living in the fullest sense of that word. Alive and vibrant in our difference—but also alive and vital in our communion with one another as we come to know who we are, as we come to know who we love, and who loves us. True religion reveals the nature of belovedness. This is the greatest and most lasting gift of community. It trains us to accept God's love.

God's love is a thing that demands everything even as it requires nothing. It demands our whole self offered in loving service, worship, and adoration for that is the only shape our lives can take as we take in and accept the fullness of God's love. A healthy community and Church can be a workshop for this spiritual work—we come to know ourselves as members of a body that knows us and yet still loves us. It is that point when artifice can be undone and grace abounds for we no longer need pretend or act out to get the attention of those we just wish would notice us. The power of community is that when it is functioning at its best, it is forming deeply self-aware and potent individuals—potent because they become aware of the grace welling up in them that yearns to take the shape of their lives as their lives take the form of living grace.

This is the consequence of true religion. It is demanding. It is rigorous. It is beautiful. It binds us together as the Church catholic. In all of that it is calling us to lives of consequence—as all lives are in God's economy. It reveals to us the essential nature of the faith and opens to us the treasury of grace. I have always had an attraction to those forms of traditional Catholic devotion that often seem a little too graphic for more restrained sensibilities. Devotions like the Sacred Heart, the Immaculate Heart, the Sorrowful Heart, the Five Wounds, and more have drawn me in.

Perhaps it is because they were around me when I grew up without being really engaged—they were symbols that were ubiquitous, like those Buddhist images in the temples that fascinated me, which I never truly understood. I believe I continue to be fascinated by them because they are so very real and transgressive. They speak to me of a faith that is deeply and achingly aware of the suffering Body all around us. This is the heart of our faith. In its sacred sorrow—in its immaculate wounds—is revealed the depths that God spans to reach us. He continues to reach for us, continues to invite us, continues to cross boundaries to know and claim us.

This is the reality that young adults are yearning for—to see and know that Christ still reaches, still lives, and still knows their joys and sorrows. A Church that can preach with love will find itself caught up in that yearning too and know itself more fully, deeply, and truly caught up in the heart of Christ.

The Contributors

Nathan Beall is currently a student at Berkley Divinity School at Yale and is the seminarian intern at Ascension in the Hill, a mission of Christ Church, New Haven. He comes from the diocese of Washington, DC, where he served at St. Mary's Parish in southern Maryland. He has interests in sustainable agriculture, pastoral ministry, community living, and ministry with the poor.

Aleithia Burgess holds degrees from Oklahoma State University and the University of Aberdeen, and has worked in education and the nonprofit sector. Her writing has appeared in *Expat Lit*, which was an online literary magazine for writers abroad. She lives in Oklahoma.

David Burman is a Canadian-American graduate of the University of Tennessee who is a member of the 2012–13 class of Saint Hilda interns. His site placement is at AIDS Project New Haven, where he coordinates the Caring Cuisine meal delivery program. He is a passionate fan of the Seattle Mariners baseball team and also loves trains.

Elizabeth Costello is a curate at St. John's Cathedral in Denver, Colorado. She studied at Yale/Berkley Divinity School and Duke Divinity School and has served as a cofounding missioner of the Community of the Franciscan Way, director of Christian formation at Holy Comforter Episcopal Church (Burlington, North Carolina), youth/children's worker at St. Peter and St. Paul Parish (Great Missenden, United Kingdom), and support worker at Lucy Faithful Homeless Hostel (Oxford, United Kingdom).

Brigid Davis Snow, from Rockland, Maine, recently graduated from Yale Law School and Yale Divinity School, concentrating in Puritan history. Far from a Puritan herself, she was raised nonreligious and converted to Christianity via Roman Catholicism. Through Christ Church, New Haven, she discovered the Anglo-Catholic tradition and sought reception into the Episcopal Church. Brigid has been at the parish for four years, becoming involved in the twenties/thirties group, parish choir, stewardship committee, and acolyte corps.

Ardath Dixon participated in Saint Hilda's House from 2011–12. She grew up in Manchester, Massachusetts, as the youngest of three. Graduating from Trinity College in Hartford with a degree in biology and religion, she then facilitated outdoor education in Center Tuftonboro, New Hampshire, after which she joined Saint Hilda's House in New Haven. Following the Episcopal Service Corps, Ardath became a public ally through AmeriCorps, continuing her service work with education reform in New Haven.

Sarah Dunn is a first-year master of divinity student at Yale Divinity School and is a postulant in the diocese of Western Massachusetts. During her discernment process, between graduating from Mount Holyoke College and beginning her seminary career, Sarah took part in the Episcopal Service Corps at Saint Hilda's House in New Haven. She has always felt a strong call to parish ministry, but after her time in the Episcopal Service Corps, an attraction to young adult ministry became part of her discernment process.

Richard "Rick" Durance is recent alumnus of University of Michigan where he studied history and worked on local interfaith organizing, especially within Lutheran and Episcopal churches. He is also an alumnus of Lutheran Volunteer Corp with San Francisco Night Ministry and Episcopal Service Corp through Saint Hilda's House in New Haven, Connecticut. He is currently part of the Ascension House community and the assistant to the executive director at Community Soup Kitchen in New Haven.

Jessica "Jessa" Fowler has followed the series of pushes and pulls that have led her from studying archaeology on the West Coast to teaching fifth grade as part of Saint Hilda's House in Connecticut to learning about farming and milking goats in the mountains of

Virginia. She thinks there's a reason Jesus spent so much of his ministry around the table and is working to build community around growing and eating food in rural Virginia.

Eric Gregory served as seminarian at Christ Church, New Haven from 2011–13, and in May 2013 received his master of divinity from Yale Divinity School. Eric hails from the Episcopal diocese of Virginia, where he is a postulant seeking holy orders. In his undergraduate career, Eric focused on pre- and postmodern British literature and film. Needless to say, Eric is a huge fan of movies and books, and he is also fond of comics, video games, cooking, and music.

The Reverend Robert (Bob) Griffith is a priest in New York City. He has worked for over twenty years with students and young adults in university and parish settings. He is the founding director of the Imago Dei Initiative (http://imagodeiinitiative.org) dedicated to understanding how best to do ministry among young people. He is a chaplain at the Pratt Institute and a priest at St. Paul's Church Carroll Street, Brooklyn.

Steve King is from Lawrence, Kansas, and is currently a seminarian at Virginia Theological Seminary, sponsored by the Episcopal diocese of Kansas. He is an alumnus of Saint Hilda's House in the Episcopal Service Corps. He lives in Alexandria, Virginia, with his wife, Ellen, where they love to travel, run and be active, spend time with friends, and explore new restaurants.

Matthew Larson is a member of Christ Church, New Haven, where he was baptized. He has been an acolyte there for several years. He is currently a college student in New Hampshire studying marine biology.

Laurel McCormack recently graduated from Mercer University in Macon, Georgia, where she got her undergraduate degree in international affairs. She spent most of her time being spoiled by tiny class sizes with compassionate professors, frequent visits from her siblings and parents, late-night grocery runs with her best friends, and ice cream trips with the Glad River congregation. She works at a refugee resettlement agency in New Haven, Connecticut, where she is one of the eleven in the Saint Hilda's House community.

Neil Raman graduated with a degree in mathematics from the University of Chicago in 2010. After completing his degree, he returned to his native Long Island and helped found a campus ministry at Stony Brook Southampton. He spent the 2012–13 academic year as a member of the Saint Hilda's House community. He is currently a postulant for Holy Orders from the diocese of Long Island and a seminarian at the School of Theology at the University of the South in Sewanee, Tennessee.

Sarah Raven, MST, MDiv., has a background in religion and education. Sarah spent four years teaching elementary school in the South Bronx. She is an alumnus of the Episcopal Service Corps–Saint Hilda's House of New Haven and currently a member of Ascension House. Sarah is the program director of GARLiC (*Green Art Recreating Life in Communities*), a green arts program that promotes a reduction in waste and art appreciation for low-income residents of the Hill (see http://garlicart.com).

The Reverend Steve Rice, SCP, is the rector of St Timothy's Episcopal Church in Winston-Salem, North Carolina, and cofounder of the Abraham Project, a member program of the Episcopal Service Corps. He is also the council advisor to the Society of Catholic Priests, a member of the Confraternity of the Blessed Sacrament, and is a priest associate of the Shrine of Our Lady of Walsingham. A lifelong Southerner, he is the husband to Cherilyn and father to Abby, Walker, and Luke. He writes for several blogs and makes his home at http://frsteverice.com.

Mason Shefa is nineteen years old and a sophomore at Yale University. Born in Minneapolis, he grew up in Los Angeles, California, where he and his family attended a conservative Presbyterian megachurch. After coming to Yale, he felt called to the Episcopal Church and was baptized and confirmed. An artist, he makes avant-garde films and composes sacred music when he isn't studying for his next exam. Ever since he can remember, he has enjoyed making films, writing poetry, and composing music.

James Shire is a first-year student attending Church Divinity School of the Pacific, an Episcopal Seminary in Berkeley, California. He is working toward a master of divinity and a master of arts with an emphasis on the history of Christianity in Asia. He is originally from Hawaii, and his first experience with an intentional community was through Saint Hilda's House, a program with the Episcopal Service Corps in 2011–12.

Carrie Staab is a Connecticut native and graduate of the College of the Holy Cross. After graduation she worked with the reconciliation ministry and Community of the Cross of Nails at Coventry Cathedral in the United Kingdom. She returned to her home state to continue the work of faith-based action in community through Saint Hilda's House. She is currently a member of the Ascension House community, working at the Loaves and Fishes food pantry and Christian Community Action in New Haven.

The Reverend Erika Takacs joined the staff of Saint Mark's, Philadelphia, as the associate rector in July 2011. Previously she served at Christ Church, Old Town Alexandria, first as a clergy resident in the Foundations for Spiritual Leadership program and then as the associate rector for faith formation and evangelism. Before graduating in 2007 from Virginia Theological Seminary, she was a high school and middle school chorus teacher in New Hope, Pennsylvania. She has also enjoyed a career as a singer specializing in early music. She holds degrees from West Chester University of Pennsylvania (1995) and Westminster Choir College (1998). Mother Takacs is a member of the Association of Anglican Musicians and is a founding member of the Society of Catholic Priests in North America. Outside of her work, her two great loves are reading and baseball.

Adam Trettel grew up in Alabama and worked at IRIS, a refugee resettlement agency in New Haven, Connecticut, as a member of Saint Hilda's House in 2011–12. Previously he earned a BA in humanities at Yale College and is currently studying for a master of theology degree at the University of Edinburgh.

Jordan Trumble is a three-time veteran of Episcopal Service Corps where she spent one year with the Episcopal Urban Intern Program and two years with Saint Hilda's House. She holds a bachelor's degree in religion from Capital University (Ohio) where she wrote her senior thesis on intentional Christian community. Currently a student at Yale Divinity School, she has done extensive work with

Episcopal summer camp ministries as well as young adult and college ministries.

Ed Watson grew up in Scotland before moving south to attend Oxford University to study philosophy and theology. Arriving as a near lifelong atheist, he found Christian faith in the middle of his second year. After completing his undergraduate degree and a postgraduate teaching qualification, he was offered a place at Saint Hilda's House, where he currently works teaching fifth graders from disadvantaged backgrounds. As well as direct service, he is especially enjoying the opportunity to see the lessons of philosophical theology manifested in the life of community.

Joseph Wolyniak is a cofounding missioner of the Community of the Franciscan Way (Durham, North Carolina), DPhil candidate at the University of Oxford, Episcopal Church Foundation Fellow, and vice chair of The Episcopal Church's Executive Council Committee on Science, Technology, and Faith.